DARK
PSYCHOLOGY
DETECTED

The All-in-One Book to Decipher Secret Deception Techniques, Discover How to Analyze People, Defeat Manipulation and Gaslighting to Protect Your Life, Money, and Freedom.

TABLE OF CONTENTS

PART IV: THE REAL DEFENSE AGAINST THE DARK ARTS

INTRODUCTION

"When you know what a man wants, you know who he is and how to move him."

- George R.R. Martin

"Know thy enemy and know yourself, and in a hundred battles, you will never be defeated."

- Sun Tzu (Art of War)

Have you ever felt coerced into doing something? Have you ever found yourself doing something and suddenly realizing that you did not know why? And worst of all, have you ever been in the horrible situation of doing something you loathed?

These instances are often the result of a pervasive problem—you have been subjected to manipulation!

If someone has been toying with your feelings, controlling you through your emotions, exploiting your weaknesses, etc., they have manipulated you.

Now you may be thinking, "I don't let people manipulate me! I make my own choices." And for the most part, that may be true. But how much do you really know about the language and techniques of manipulation? Could you even recognize manipulation if you saw it?

Manipulation leaves us feeling controlled, sad, and unsure of ourselves. Constant manipulation can cause us to handle an entire gamut of negative emotions ranging from wrath, frustration, confusion, and grief to abject hopelessness.

Psychological manipulation can feel so demeaning and denigrating that we may wonder how we missed such a devious assault.

And yet, could you have prevented it if you had been aware? The answer is a resounding yes. Awareness of a problem is the first step to finding a solution. The most famous line from the Art of War talks about the importance of knowledge in achieving victory.

Knowing the enemy is vital to defeating it. And psychological manipulation is undoubtedly an enemy. It is a despicable foe that erodes that unique ability that makes us complete human beings. That beautiful thing, which separates humans from all other species, is AGENCY. Agency is the best word to describe what is destroyed by psychological manipulation.

Clearly understanding what the word agency means in this context is essential. Agency here refers to the capacity of an individual to exert power or influence. Your agency is what gives you the wherewithal to control your own life. It gives you the discretion necessary to live your life to its fullest.

Control is evidence of an autonomous and free individual. Historically, a lack of control was common in enslaved people worldwide. Ethnicity, culture, race, space, and time did not matter because slavery had one defining feature. Slaves did not control their own lives.

Hence, if anybody today lacks this complete control over their own lives, can they be regarded as free? Suppose they lack the agency to decide what is good for them. Then, are they all that different from the unjustly enslaved people who existed throughout history?

According to the American Psychological Association (APA), psychology studies the human mind, how it works, and how it affects human behavior. The APA also defines psychological manipulation as behavior designed to exploit, control, or otherwise influence others to one's advantage.

This nefarious practice of psychological manipulation is popularly called Dark Psychology and is the book's subject.

We have all been subjected to various forms of influence and coercion. It is not incorrect to think that every human being born on this planet has been manipulated in one way or another. Likewise, every one of us has been influenced by someone else.

Influence or the action of controlling another human being comes in various forms. Words like persuasion or coercion allude to what influence truly is: power. Power affects the capacities, acts, beliefs, or conduct of others.

Dark Psychology is the exercise of power that exploits others unethically for the benefit of the exploiter. It is hence Dark Power.

Whether we call it dark psychology, dark power, or psychological manipulation, it is incumbent upon us to learn as much as possible about it. If everyone experiences manipulation to varying degrees, it is evident that the only truly free people are those who are reasonably immune to psychological manipulation.

Why? We enjoy true freedom only when our actions are genuinely our own and not when they result from someone else's influence. We must understand that on paper, every human being has certain "inalienable rights," or "natural rights," or whatever they might be called. Universal human rights is a magnificent concept. But when subjected to psychological manipulation, we do not enjoy our rights fully.

In 2021 alone, the total financial losses caused by manipulative crimes were estimated to be over 1 trillion dollars. That's more money than the GDPs of 180 countries in the world!

It is estimated that 50-80% of adults are subjected to emotional abuse from psychological manipulation. That is around 5 billion people!

And this is why this book was written. This work aims to teach people how they can discover, decipher, and defeat dark psychology. For this, we will rely on the most prodigiously studied concepts of psychological manipulation. This book was created by combining impactful scientific insights with irrefutable facts from real-world experiences.

Dark Psychology Detected includes an amalgamation of content from peer-reviewed academic journals and highly prestigious magazines. These include Pew Research, Harvard Business Review, Psychology Today, Hypatia, American Sociological Review, the APA, etc.

However, this book does not merely assert what psychological manipulation is. It does much more. It is divided into four sections. Part one will focus on the traditional science of dark psychology and examine the various signs indicating the existence of manipulation.

Part Two will shed light on some individuals' evil exercise of power over others. This exercise is the traditional area of study regarding psychological manipulation. Part Two will thus show how typical nefarious individuals prey on others using dark psychology.

Part Three, on the other hand, will look at mass manipulation. This book section will be even more critical because it deals with a more significant power imbalance. We will look at the differences between persuasion and manipulation, which will prove incredibly crucial later.

Mass manipulation is even more malicious than individual manipulation because it deals with manipulation on a colossal scale, including a global level. This part of the book shows how billions of people worldwide are controlled by vile manipulative techniques that have become even more powerful with advanced technologies.

Devious digital technological devices have enabled collective entities like corporations, governments, media organizations, politicians, etc., to indulge in deception like never before! Artifice refers to clever or cunning devices or methods, especially those used to trick or deceive others.

These machinations also allow these already powerful groups to control the lives of ordinary people to an almost inconceivable extent.

Now, it is worth considering the ramifications of psychological manipulation. People abused by dark psychology may feel used and depressed and may lose all sense of hope and self-worth. But what is even more damning is that they stand to lose more than their emotional well-being.

Psychological Manipulation can result in innocent people losing their money, wasting their time, and even failing at relationships. Dark Psychology is used to extort money from us. Manipulators waste our time making us do things that benefit them but harm us.

Targets of Dark Psychology usually end up having their lives ruined. It is this despicable characteristic that inspired the creation of this book. It is indeed the most crucial part of the book: Defeating Dark Psychology.

In Part Four, we have developed the real Defense Against the Dark Arts (pardon the Harry Potter reference). Part Four deals with resisting manipulation. This section will go through the various practices that help ordinary people like us acquire significant immunity against dark psychology.

This part is where the author's experience and expertise really come into play. The author is educated in psychology, business, sociology, and power. In addition, he also graduated in computer engineering, which allowed him to explore the immense propensity of digital tech to be used for malicious purposes.

This book uses what is taught in universities, business schools, and sales and marketing lessons to reverse-engineer the effects of manipulation devices to find the best ways to counter them. Instead of slogging through dense research papers, you'll get a simple, to-the-point explanation of the information you most need to know.

But how will that benefit you? First, you can expect to save money and buy only what you desire. Second, you can protect yourself from great unhappiness. Third, you can improve your health. Finally, you can reduce the stress in your life, boost your longevity, and become happier.

You can also improve your chances of recognizing malevolent individuals and stop yourself from being victimized in the first place. Imagine all the trouble, pain, and losses you could avoid by never being manipulated in the first place. Less pain inevitably leads to more happiness.

Though the odds are more heavily stacked against the individual citizen now than ever before, we have discovered new ways to counter even the most egregious forms of advanced manipulation.

The book will help you achieve the happiness few people have attained. Everybody is manipulated in one way or another, and freedom comes from being immune to manipulation. In that case, it is imperative to counter manipulation. This is because only the free can live fulfilling lives, which means that real happiness stems from self-realizing, self-actualizing, and objective success.

When you have control over your own life, you can begin to better yourself, optimize your existence, choose your friends correctly, do great things and achieve your goals and desires.

In other words, the road to real happiness starts with the ability to resist manipulation and thus make our lives truly our own.

Let us now get into the thick of it and take a hard look at the enemy. But, first, we shall learn what manipulation is all about.

PART I

DARK PSYCHOLOGY:

SIGNS & SCIENCE!

CHAPTER ONE
UNCOVERING MANIPULATION

The APA defines psychological manipulation as behavior designed to exploit, control, or otherwise influence others to one's advantage. Henceforth, this book will use manipulation to refer to psychological manipulation unless otherwise stated.

Interestingly, the Merriam-Webster dictionary states that manipulation is to control or play upon by artful, unfair, or insidious means, especially to one's advantage. Trickery, pressure, and focusing on the victim's reasoning faculty are considered standard manipulation devices. (*Noggle, 2020*)

Suppose we combine these two sources of information. In that case, we can define manipulation as behavior designed to control others for personal benefit through unethical and immoral practices. It is insidious and evil. This understanding is crucial for a correct analysis of manipulation.

Well then, why is it so prevalent? Why do so many people engage in manipulation? This exploration exposes several unpleasant truths. Human beings are mortal. Our lives are limited. Because of this, we are often conditioned to seek the easiest and most efficient way to achieve our goals.

Time is our most valuable resource. Therefore, saving time is one of the primary drivers behind every optimization decision we make. Furthermore, it implies that people will look for the easiest solution to whatever problems they want to resolve.

Optimal and efficient problem resolution is a noble endeavor that deserves applause. However, there is a big difference when amoral and immoral people pursue such endeavors. Psychological manipulation involves deceptive and exploitative techniques, frequently utilized by individuals who exhibit one or more of the negative personality qualities outlined in the next chapter.

Immoral people do not shrink from hurting others in pursuit of their personal goals. But, even more tellingly, some people enjoy harming others and profiting in the process.

Hence, psychological manipulation can be a malicious means to achieve personal ends. It can also be a nefarious end in itself because the perpetrator enjoys the feeling of manipulating someone. The former is more common than the latter, but it is no less damaging to the person being controlled.

People thus use manipulation because an intended goal requires specific actions to be performed by others. For example, businesses need profit, which means exchanging money for goods of "perceived value." In a free country, this exchange of goods is the foundation of economics and of society itself, and it is supposedly "voluntary".

Manipulation is also used to obtain desired objectives in relationships. For example, in an intimate relationship, one person may indulge in manipulative actions to get their partner to provide something.

Providing intimacy for money or other benefits and vice versa can be a form of manipulation. In fact, it is one of the oldest forms of manipulation. It is not just the "oldest profession." Consent may very well be provided, but it may not be all that "informed" or all that "freely given."

At this stage, we must understand that all forms of influence are not inherently evil, nor are they intended to provide benefits only to the influencer. There is even the opposite kind of influence where the influencing person will be sacrificing their personal interests to make things better for the party being influenced.

This is most commonly seen in filial and familial relationships, especially in the case of parents. Parents will often compromise their own interests for the benefit of their children. This stems from the concept that parents' "selfish" interests do indeed include their children. The idea that children are parents' most prized possession has led to society's success.

Parental influence over their children is not considered malignant and is often something to be desired instead. When competent teachers influence their students, the outcome is not intended to be negative. When good leaders lead their followers, or when capable managers and bosses influence their subordinates in a good way, the influence is not evil. On the contrary, it could very well be the best thing for society.

An organized, meritocratic hierarchy can be the very essence of order and the antithesis of chaos. In other words, power is not inherently wrong. On the contrary, it could very well be an honorable thing if used correctly. Every parent understands using bribery to persuade their kids to eat vegetables.

Yet, when it comes to adults, influencing can become a compulsion. This, in turn, becomes manipulation if the other party is harmed or subjected to any form of loss. The difference here is that the intentions of the influencer are relevant. It is manipulation if the manipulated person's liberty, agency, and free choice are infringed upon, and that person comes to harm.

It would be valuable now to approach this concept with the help of an analogous concept. Consider then the idea of "spoils." Spoils of war is a term used to describe any property acquired during the fog of war. In reality, it is nothing but war looting/raiding. Manipulation, similarly, is done to steal things that belong to others.

Some women use their charms to manipulate weak-minded men into doing things that would cause harm in various ways. Manipulation knows no gender. While the modes and methods of manipulation may change, the principle always remains the same—unethical behavior designed to insidiously influence another person for your benefit, often at their cost.

As society became more modern, violent conflict and physical theft of goods became crimes, subjected to judicial punishment if convicted. This criminalization of theft is, of course, warranted and indisputable. Even during wars between nations, the threat of war crimes prosecution can negate the baser urges of the people fighting.

Today, stealing is considered evil by all law-abiding citizens and moral people. Theft is frowned upon by civilized human beings. However, the concept of law-and-order does not account for the transfer of ownership done through psychological manipulation. This immoral transfer is not considered illegal. Technically, it shouldn't even be made illegal. This drawback is the heinous brilliance of it.

Individual sovereignty, the bedrock of freedom in the modern world, drives the idea of individual liberty. Individual sovereignty can best be understood as self-ownership, where a person is considered to have the moral right to have bodily integrity and be the sole controller of their life. Physical force and violence should not be used to negate this freedom. It is a violation of universal human rights. Individual sovereignty works on the concept that everybody is equal under the law, capable of self-ownership, and is thus responsible for their actions.

However, this does not account for the fact that people can be influenced by ideas and thoughts, which are the drivers of psychological manipulation. Since physical force is not used, psychological manipulation cannot be considered illegal either. The unfortunate truth is that many evil people desist from criminal behavior only because of the deterrent aspect of a robust judicial system. In other words, the costs of indulging in evil outweigh the benefits.

Combining all the ideas explained so far, we come to the following conclusion. Manipulation can provide favorable outcomes to the perpetrators, and it is not illegal. In other words, manipulators can commit evil and get away with it!

This is why this book has been written. People seldom have access to legal recourse when they have been oppressed through manipulation. They have to take action on their own. We have had a superficial look at manipulation and why it is usually done. Let us now take a brief look at how manipulation is typically exercised.

It has already been explained how dark psychology attempts to overcome the agency of its victims. This agency provides individuals control over themselves and is directly connected to our senses and awareness. Therefore, it is indisputable that psychological manipulation works best by countering this sense of awareness. (*King, 2013*)

Manipulation must be subtle and indirect enough to avoid being noticed by the perpetrator's prey. In other cases, there is such an enormous power imbalance between the perpetrator and their target that apparently, the victim cannot do anything about it.

The takeaway is that power imbalances are often at the root of many instances of manipulation. Manipulators work to create a power imbalance. Manipulators will hide their tactics and disguise their hostile intentions to bypass potential resistance from their victims subtly.

Many will spend significant time getting to know us and our weaknesses and identifying the best ways to overcome our resistance. However, this also means that just because we have known someone for a particular length of time, it in no way indicates that this person will not manipulate us. The most skillful manipulators often spring their trap only after we have placed our trust in them.

At this juncture, we must remember that manipulators can appear kind. It is good to be aware of this fact, especially if we notice them being cruel to others. It is invaluable knowledge. If we observe someone manipulating another person, they may do the same to us. Therefore, we must be on guard against such a manipulative individual.

On this note of caution, let us focus more on the "How" behind psychological manipulation. How is dark psychology enacted? What are the main tactics and techniques used by the perpetrators?

Usually, most techniques of inter-personal manipulation are designed to create three particular emotional reactions in the manipulators' intended victims.

Fear, obligation, and Guilt

Manipulators use emotional, psychological, and physical tactics to get what they want by creating an imbalance of power, as described above. But, this imbalance of power is commonly made by creating particular emotions in the targets. In psychological manipulation, emotions are often the most easily used tool to subjugate the intended target. The three most common emotions that manipulators try to instill in their prey are fear, a sense of obligation, and a feeling of guilt.

Manipulators use these emotions to exploit their victims to gain power, control, benefits, or privileges. This state of affairs is often called toxic manipulation.

Two of the most prevalent manipulator types are "the bully" and "the victim." (*Psychology Today, 2017*). A bully instills fear in you and may use anger, threats, and intimidation to exert control over you. Bullying is thematically similar to the violent offenders of pre-modern history.

The "victim," on the other hand, creates a sense of guilt in the target. The "victim" frequently feigns pain or loss and may subtly indicate that their prey is responsible for their state. However, while manipulators often portray themselves as victims, the fact is that they are the people who have caused the situation and are usually in control.

Only yesterday, a friend of ours, Felicia, mentioned how she was subjected to a bizarre experience. When someone provided a sub-par performance (including plagiarism) on a test she had paid for on a website, Felicia rightfully chose to eliminate the offender from contention.

However, the candidate then began to talk about how the rejection would affect their rating on the online platform. She then used this pity appeal to convince Felicia that she should either select them or give them another chance. Felicia told us how she felt terribly guilty for rejecting them.

Fortunately for her, Felicia held her ground and went through the process of rejecting the candidate. But, she did feel terrible about it and even felt guilty. She said that the whole episode went against her good nature.

This inherent "niceness" that some people exude is often the target of manipulators pretending to be victims. A person approached by victim-manipulators frequently tries to assist the manipulator in an attempt to relieve their feeling of guilt.

Targets of this type of manipulation frequently feel obligated to assist the victim by doing anything to ease their distress. (Psychology Today, 2017). An obligation is created through guilt, and the accompanying 'sense of duty' is a potent device that the manipulator would gleefully target.

The flip side of using the obligation-guilt process can also be manipulative. Kindness can be a form of manipulation. A random act of kindness can create a powerful sense of obligation. This process depends on the person doing the persuading and their intention. In fact, in a subsequent chapter, we will see how this precise form of kindness is a potent, real-life manipulation device.

Manipulative acts of kindness may be used by abusers when seeking forgiveness. Emotional manipulation is often seen in intimate relationships where the perpetrators might pledge never to hurt their victims again. They may attempt to make the repentance tangible by buying something material to "compensate" their victims for the pain they have inflicted.

Persistent manipulation, evidenced by a consistent habit of abusive actions followed by contrite kindness, is not genuine remorse; it is abuse. Moreover, this deceptive friendliness and any emotional manipulation may appear quite perplexing to the victim since it leaves a person wondering about what is happening in the relationship.

This state of confusion could be what the manipulator desires because it makes further manipulation more likely to succeed. A confused victim is rendered incapable of defending themselves appropriately. It creates that power imbalance we have highlighted several times before.

Two questions can arise here:

- Is it bad to be kind to someone, so they are more willing to help you?
- Where do you draw the line?

Here is an example. When dating, it's usually assumed that the other person presents themselves at their best and downplays their bad habits to make a good impression. Would this be considered manipulation? It could be. (Noggle, 2020)

Let us unravel this complexity by going deeper into some more manipulation techniques.

Tactics of toxic manipulation

1. Location advantage

A manipulative person will try to pull you away from your comfort zone and away from places you are comfortable with to gain an advantage over you. The purpose is for the manipulator to have more control at the expense of the prey. (*Shortsleeve, 2018*)

2. Manipulation of facts

A manipulator will lie to others, find excuses, accuse, or strategically divulge information about themselves while withholding other facts. They think they are gaining control and intellectual superiority by doing so. (*Aberson, 2019*) Disinformation and propaganda are among the most successful manipulation tools ever devised by mankind.

Objective reality exists, but some people may perceive reality differently. Manipulators can prevent their victims from accurately experiencing reality because perception depends on the individual's senses and cognitive capabilities.

3. Exaggeration and generalization

Exaggeration and generalization are standard tools of manipulators. For example, one of the phrases you will hear them say in conversations is, "No one ever loved me." This is intended to evoke pity and sympathy. However, they also have the additional purpose of lowering the victim's guard, opening them up for more ruthless manipulation.

Manipulators utilize ambiguous allegations to obscure the flaws in their claims. (*Shortsleeve, 2018*). This can occur in general discourse, too, and this is precisely what happened in Felicia's example. A work not given acceptance would not have affected the perpetrator's rating on the website. Since they resorted to plagiarism, they deserved to be penalized anyway. Despite all that, their hyperbole (exaggeration) successfully evoked sympathy and guilt.

Trivialization and over-exaggeration are methods used to obscure the reality of events and objects. It hinders the victim's ability to correctly and accurately grasp the truth. This faulty comprehension prevents the victim from acquiring knowledge—the first weapon to counter any enemy, including manipulation.

4. Cruel humor

Manipulators utilize this method to exploit weaknesses and make people feel vulnerable. They gain feelings of supremacy by making others appear awful.

Many bullies often attempt to reconcile and justify their actions, claiming they were only joking. Even if it were true, it is irrelevant. Their claim only makes their actions more egregious. If their humor involves bullying somebody, it clearly shows their evil nature. In retrospect, this kind of humor is a great indicator one can use to identify potentially manipulative and despicable individuals.

5. Gaslighting

The manipulator uses this technique to confound people and get them to doubt their own reality. Then, when people address the abuse or misinformation, the manipulator assures them that it never occurred. This form of perspective manipulation is a well-researched type of manipulation, made famous by the eponymous 1944 movie, whose name is now used to refer to this particular type of coercion: Gaslighting. This topic will be discussed in more detail in its own chapter.

6. Passive-aggression

Humans can be passive-aggressive for various reasons, and manipulation needn't be the driver in most instances. However, deliberate manipulators will apply this method by indulging in passive hostility and avoiding direct confrontation (for example, the silent treatment). They're doing this to convey displeasure without openly expressing it. (*Shortsleeve, 2018*). As a result, the targets of this type of manipulation often feel exasperated, drained, and confused. They may also suffer from bouts of anxiety. This effect usually stems from the clear distinction between what the victim observes and what the devious manipulator communicates.

7. Spurious judging

Manipulators do not always disguise their manipulation under a layer of humor or "good fun." Instead, they may openly condemn, insult, and discard people with deliberate intent. In this scenario, they want the chosen prey to believe they are doing something wrong.

Also, it is vital to note that no matter what the target does, they will fall short of the manipulator's expectations. The perpetrators only address the negative things in the situation and may not provide positive answers. (*Shortsleeve, 2018*)

Because the motivations for manipulation might range from mild to severe, it is critical to accurately assess the circumstances under which the manipulation occurs. Unfortunately, this can be extremely difficult due to a lack of control over the conditions that need to be examined. (*Chester, 2021*)

This difficulty means that we must always be aware of the context before we can ascertain the motivation of the manipulator with any reasonable certainty. But that is a challenging thing to do. This is why it is so difficult to counter psychological manipulation.

This chapter turned out to be massive, but that was necessary. Knowing the basics of manipulation is essential to be better positioned when learning about the more detailed processes associated with dark psychology.

On that note, let's consider a cognitive skill that plays a decisive role in the study of all things, including psychological manipulation. That skill is pattern recognition. Pattern recognition is the most sought-after tool in intellectual discourse. IQ tests attach value to pattern recognition skills because these skills are a sign of high-functioning cognitive competencies.

It just so happens that pattern recognition can also be used to examine psychological manipulation. One area where this is done is in the study of the patterns in the personality traits found in dark psychology perpetrators.

Can you spot a manipulator by their personality? It turns out that many people who manipulate others share some common traits, although they aren't always immediately apparent. In the next chapter, you'll learn about these traits and how they manifest.

References:

American Psychological Association: APA Dictionary: "manipulation."

Aberson, C. L. (2019). Applied power analysis for the behavioral sciences. New York, NY: Routledge.

Contributors, W. M. D. E. (n.d.). Manipulation: 7 signs to look for. WebMD. Retrieved April 14, 2022, from https://www.webmd.com/mental-health/signs-manipulation

Chester, D. S., & Lasko, E. N. (2021). Construct Validation of Experimental Manipulations in Social Psychology: Current Practices and Recommendations for the Future. Perspectives on Psychological Science, 16(2), 377–395. https://doi.org/10.1177/1745691620950684

King, M. (2013). The problem with manipulation. Ethics, 124(1), 65-83.

Rudinow, J. (1978). Manipulation. Ethics, 88(4), 338-347.

Noggle, Robert, "The Ethics of Manipulation", The Stanford Encyclopedia of Philosophy (Summer 2020 Edition), Edward N. Zalta (ed.)

Shortsleeve, C. (2018, October 16). How to Tell if Someone Is Manipulating You - And What to Do About It. Retrieved from TIME: https://time.com/5411624/how-to-tell-if-being-manipulated/

https://www.psychologytoday.com/ca/blog/toxic-relationships/201704/are-you-being-manipulated

Key Chapter One Takeaways

1. Manipulation is the practice of controlling others through insidious and immoral ways for selfish interests, which often causes harm to the manipulated.

2. Time is the most important resource available to human beings. Manipulation is done for two reasons—firstly, to gain advantages in the easiest way, regardless of who gets hurt, and secondly, because some people just enjoy manipulating others.

3. Manipulation is used because the perpetrator needs the victims to do something for the perpetrator's benefit.

4. Manipulation is pervasive and prevalent because the manipulator can get away with it.

5. Manipulation often works by creating power imbalances between the perpetrators and their targets.

6. Dark Psychology works by exploiting the weaknesses of the intended victims, and thus manipulators might initially appear friendly to their targets.

7. Three common emotional reactions targeted by manipulators include fear, obligation, and guilt.

8. Tactics of Toxic manipulation include —location advantage, manipulation of facts, cruel humor, gaslighting, exaggeration and generalization, spurious judging, etc.

9. Pattern recognition can be an immense aid in detecting dark psychology, and certain personality types have been found to be common among manipulators. This will be discussed in the next chapter.

CHAPTER TWO

THE DARK TRIAD:
A RECIPE FOR MANIPULATION?

If you had to pick three traits to describe yourself, what would they be? Hopefully, not any of the ones you'll discover in this chapter. Read on to learn the traits that many master manipulators embody.

The Dark Triad is the infamous three traits often associated with Dark Psychology and Manipulation. The Dark Triad refers to a trio of potentially harmful personality traits and was famously coined by researchers Delroy L. Paulhus and Kevin M. Williams in 2002. These are Machiavellianism, Narcissism, and Psychopathy. (*Paulhus & Williams, 2002*)

To completely understand the Dark Triad, one must first understand the Personality Assessment Criteria known as the Big 5. Many studies have used this criterion to complement the original research information on Dark Triad traits. Therefore, learning about the Big 5 paradigm is valuable because it helps one understand the Dark Triad better. The Big 5 Personality Test is a five-factor model of core personality traits that have proven vital to understanding the nature and features of evil individuals.

Over several decades, these five categories have been thoroughly investigated and tested. Let us now delve into these traits in detail.

- **Openness**

Openness, also known as openness to experience, is a fundamental personality characteristic that indicates receptivity to new ideas and experiences. People who are open to new experiences are more likely to seek a range of adventures. They would be more comfortable with the unexpected and pay attention to their inner sensations than those who are not. They have a strong desire to learn new things and like being surprised. People who score low on openness favor habits, people, and familiar ideas; they may be closed-minded.

- **Conscientiousness**

Conscientiousness is a fundamental personality trait that can best be understood as a combination of dedication and dutifulness. A conscientious person is responsible, organized, hardworking, goal-oriented, and follows rules and conventions. This trait is most closely associated with righteousness and is often antithetical to the Dark Triad traits.

Conscientiousness encompasses self-control, industriousness, responsibility, and reliability (*Big 5 Personality Traits, 2022*). This could be the one trait that can be seen as the primary antagonist against malevolence. Put another way; this is the trait we should seek to find in all people we wish to network with.

Self-control and impulse control are skills that a conscientious person should possess. This personality feature can determine whether you will plan and achieve long-term objectives, mull over decisions, act cautiously, and take your responsibilities seriously.

Conscientiousness is a critical component of success in both love and business. It is also a significant predictor of health, happiness, and lifespan. It is, therefore, a trait that must be encouraged at all costs.

- **Extraversion**

Extraversion is a personality characteristic typically marked by gregariousness, intense energy and can include a penchant for talking *(Big 5 Personality Traits, 2022)*. In addition, the phrase generally refers to a condition in which someone prefers being with others. Introversion, on the other hand, is best defined as a desire to seek isolation and to choose to be alone.

- **Agreeableness**

Agreeableness measures a person's ability to be conformable and social. Cooperation, politeness, kindness, and friendliness are all personality traits regarded as agreeable. People with a high level of agreeableness are more trusting, loving, altruistic, and generally more prosocial than others (*Big 5 Personality Traits, 2022*).

People with high levels of this prosocial feature can be incredibly empathetic, exhibiting considerable care for the well-being of others, and are often the first to assist those in need.

This trait is sometimes a good indicator of the likelihood of someone being malevolent or not. The Dark Triad traits are often strongly associated with people with low agreeableness levels.

This makes logical sense because low values in this trait could imply an unreasonable hatred for others and an unnaturally selfish disposition. This disregard for others is considered a must for a manipulator since being considerate may hinder someone's ability to enact malice.

Nevertheless, you must understand that low agreeableness is not the sole judge of manipulative behavior. On the contrary, there are indeed many people who are exceptionally low in agreeableness but are, in fact, vehemently opposed to manipulation.

- **Neuroticism**

Neuroticism is characterized by intense expressions of emotions, including negative ones, like worry, despair, self-doubt, etc. Neuroticism, like other personality qualities, exists on a scale — some people are far more neurotic than others. Neuroticism is also referred to as low emotional health or negative emotionalism in the framework of the Big 5. High neuroticism could indicate low emotional health, manifesting as negative emotionalism. *(Big 5 Personality Traits, 2022)*

Although some self-deprecating entertainers and ranters may wear their neuroticism as a badge of pride, neurotic people are more prone to the debilitating effects of anxiety, mood disorders, and other adverse social and emotional outcomes.

Individual personalities feature each of these traits in varying higher and lower degrees. The exploration of the Dark Triad concept will focus on manipulative, exploitative traits that the Big 5 model does not directly explain. This book will then combine the two models to obtain a more perspicacious (clever) and perspicuous (clear) insight into dark psychology.

And now- the Dark Triad up close.

The Dark Triad

Some researchers used a particular individual scale to measure each Dark Triad trait using a 12-item questionnaire. This scale is called the "Dirty Dozen" and was released in 2010 by Jonason and Gregory Webster of the University of West Florida.

The statements (items 1-4 test Machiavellianism, items 5-8 measure Psychopathy, and items 9-12 measure Narcissism) are graded on a scale of 1 (strongly disagree) to 7 (strongly agree). The higher the score, the more likely Dark Triad inclinations are present.

These twelve questions might appear trivial, and their purpose might seem inconsequential. As such, self-reported tests like these have limitations, but denying their efficacy would be erroneous. They are exceedingly helpful. This will be explained in more detail later. For now, the twelve questions are as follows.

The twelve statements:–Dirty Dozen

1. I always manipulate others because I want it my way.

2. I have lied and deceived people before to get my way.

3. I used and still use flattery to get it my way.

4. I exploit other people.

5. I often lack remorse.

6. I am not concerned with the morality of each action I make.

7. I am usually insensitive or callous.

8. I am often cynical.

9. I often want other people to admire me.

10. I want other people to pay attention to me quite often.

11. I seek prestige or status in many situations.

12. I want other people to offer me special favors.

People with these traits are likelier to be callous and manipulative. They tend never to experience feelings of regret or remorse. They often have an unjustly inflated view of themselves. Combined with an absolute disregard for the possible negative consequences of their actions, they exhibit explicit malevolent behavior. They are also more likely to be impulsive and demonstrate a generally lower level of overt anxiety than "normal" people.

People with these Dark Triad characteristics are often ruthless and manipulative, prepared to do or say almost anything to obtain what they want. They have scant concern for others and are frequently shameless in their self-promotion.

Their inherent impulsivity can lead them to engage in risky behavior — in some situations, even to commit crimes — without thinking about the consequences of their actions. Unfortunately, this also leads to disastrous outcomes for their victims. Still, the perpetrators do not care about this aspect of their efforts.

Many academics regard psychopathy, narcissism, and Machiavellianism as three different qualities with overlapping features. However, others argue that the similarities point to an underlying personality trait that is still unknown.

Now that we have a basic idea of the Dark Triad, let us examine the three Dark Triad traits in more detail.

- **Psychopathy**

Psychopathy, a feature marked by a lack of empathy and remorse, is considered by most academics to be the "darkest" of the Dark Triad. Psychopaths often inflict more harm to individuals and society than narcissists or "High Machs."

The term "psychopath" is not a mental health diagnosis. Antisocial-personality-disorder is the disease that most closely resembles it in the APA's Diagnostic and Statistical Manual of Mental Disorders.

Yet, if there is a single scientific term that the layman can comprehend as the sure indicator of outright evil, it would be psychopathy. Psychopaths are those whose actions most clearly depict an absolute lack of righteousness. Many of the most infamous serial killers have also been found to be psychopaths. (*Cleckley, 2016*)

Hervey M. Cleckley's decades-spanning work on studying psychopathy has proven exceptionally important in our ability to understand this nefarious behavior and mindset. Even the often-used and misused idea of "masking" is entirely appropriate in the study of psychopathy. Cleckley's book is titled the Mask of Sanity. Everybody who wants to know more details about psychopathy should read that book. This book is going to apply the insights of Cleckley's book to derive uses from them.

If the occasion calls for it, it would not be imprudent to consider tolerating narcissists and even people high in Machiavellian tendencies. However, any favorable treatment of a psychopath is an exercise in futility and could even prove fatal.

Psychopaths lack any principles or morals. It has also been found that psychopathy can have physiological causes, including brain malformations. In other words, psychopathy can often be incurable and should not be tolerated.

The cause of psychopathy is not as relevant as its existence when detecting and defeating manipulation. Consequently, it is wise to never associate with or condone a psychopath.

- **Machiavellianism**

Machiavellianism is a personality attribute that describes a manipulative person who may deceive and fool others to attain goals. This label indicates a disposition where achieving a purpose at all costs is prevalent.

Machiavellianism is not a mental health diagnosis. Instead, it is based on Niccolo Machiavelli's work of political theory, The Prince, from the sixteenth century. According to some studies, Machiavellianism is the dark characteristic most strongly linked to high intelligence.

This makes sense as it is not plausible for people with low intelligence to manipulate people regularly and successfully. Artifice is an activity that requires a significant "cognitive load," as some call it.

When someone speaks of a person as a "High Mach," they refer to their Machiavellian ability to manipulate others. However, it is perhaps crucial to note that ability is not the only metric that will cause Machiavellian people to indulge in deception.

Every human being has abilities that they can choose to act upon. In this case, Machiavellian people possess the competence and the inclination to practice deception and enjoy the fruits of their devious labor.

- **Narcissism**

Narcissism, the third component of the Dark Triad triangle, is characterized by undeservedly excessive self-esteem and arrogance. When they aren't given the particular attention they feel they deserve, severe or "malignant" narcissists can become extremely abusive or violent.

Yet again, we can see that such a disposition is best expressed when the perpetrator has no regard for others. Unjustified self-interest, arising from an incorrect self-assessment, gets coupled with an affliction that seeks constant affirmation from people within their vicinity, resulting in a malignant narcissist.

Although these three personality traits are diverse in their presentation and origins, they have several characteristics in common. To varying degrees, all three features could manifest in evil characters whose behaviors tend to harm others, sometimes for self-promotion and sometimes for pleasure. They are also likely to be emotionally cold, duplicitous, and aggressive. Understanding the Dark Triad could hence prove crucial for detecting manipulation.

Over the years, many studies have been conducted to learn about the Dark Triad and Big 5 Personality traits. A famous study done in 2002 proved instrumental in teaching us ways to identify potential manipulators. (*Paulhus & Williams, 2002*)

This study used a sufficiently large sample of 245 students and measured personality and cognitive capacity. Thus, they could correlate data across different metrics and found several valuable insights.

While the three Dark Triad traits are expressed differently, they shared one concept on the Big 5 Personality Scale. All three traits of psychopathy, narcissism, and Machiavellianism shared a typically low amount of Agreeableness.

The study also showed that both psychopathy and Machiavellianism displayed low conscientiousness. But, Psychopathy alone showed low neuroticism as well. An enlightening factor is that consistent narcissism was the trait most strongly correlated with intelligence. Thus high intelligence by itself is not a sign of a manipulative person.

And this is what brings us to the invaluable conclusion of this chapter. Be aware of people who are disagreeable and not overtly sensitive (low neuroticism). But beware mainly of the person who is not conscientious.

And if you know this person is also intelligent, the warning signals must thunder loud in your mind. Stay on guard. If this person is not moral and righteous, then the facts are clear. Avoid such people if you can; if you cannot, always be cautious around them.

Several other tests showed that these Dark Triad traits are found more often in males than females. This should come as no surprise since the Dark Triad complex is a hyper-exaggerated form of competitiveness. It should also explain why Dark Triad personalities are commonly found in the corporate workspace.

There is even some evidence of companies actively seeking and recruiting personnel because they showed Dark Triad characteristics. Why on earth would companies do that? The answer can best be understood when you realize that companies desire profit and success above everything else. Dark Triad traits often indicate a greater potential for individual success.

We have already discussed how Dark Triads show low agreeableness and neuroticism. But what does that mean in real life? In essence, individuals with high levels of these dark traits appear to operate in highly selfish and competitive ways with a common core of being success-driven. The differentiating factor is that "Dark Triaders" do not have any inhibitions in hurting others to get their way.

One study claims that the common feature of the traits is callousness, or a lack of empathy towards others, which plays out differently due to the unique features of each characteristic.

- Narcissists have no regard for people they treat poorly to gain admiration.
- Machiavellians take advantage of others strategically.
- Psychopaths are usually impulsive and go after what they want without caring who gets hurt.

The science behind evil?

Regarding psychopathy, according to research, when people with psychopathic features see other people in distress or try to learn the consequences of their actions, the areas of the brain responsible for emotional processing, empathizing, and decision-making such as the amygdala, insula, and the ventromedial prefrontal cortex showed decreased activity.

In other words, individuals with psychopathy have impaired functioning in these areas of the brain. This affects their ability to form accurate connections between stimuli and repercussions, such as hurting people (stimuli) and getting punished (repercussions). Decreased activity in those brain parts hampers necessary emotional reactions and decision-making.

Research has suggested that narcissism and salary are positively correlated, while Machiavellianism is linked to career advancement. However, in the case of people with intense Dark Triad traits and a lack of morals, this success often comes at a cost to others. In such cases, the Dark Triad traits are associated with unethical behavior, white-collar crime, lying, deception, etc.

How can you know if someone has dark triad traits?

People with dark triad personalities (DTers) can be challenging to identify because they can be charismatic and charming. They are masters of false praises and excel at making others feel unique and privileged to be in their company. DTers appear to be people with superior taste, knowledge, and compassion.

People with a dark triad personality cannot maintain this impression indefinitely. It takes a significant mental effort to present a facade. They eventually destroy relationships by abusing others with whom they form intimate bonds. Some of these social failures may include the following.

- **A failure to maintain long-term relationships**

This includes romantic relationships and friends, family, and co-workers. "Dark Triaders" could have a run of failed relationships where they've "shut off" crucial people in their lives.

- **A history of being a "victim" in relationships and life**

People who have a Dark Triad personality can be masters of the typical nefarious cycle of abuse and gaslighting. They may immediately flip the script and pretend to be the victim when confronted.

- **Their stories have inconsistencies**

While they may be experts at manipulating facts to their advantage, they cannot maintain their flawless facade for a long time. As a result, some details and background information about their life are contradictory and do not add up.

This could be the easiest way to spot a manipulating DTer. However, it requires us to be highly observant and have a good memory of events. Often, this lack of clarity in our memory makes us doubt ourselves.

- **A persistent demand that must be met**

DTers must constantly be satisfied at the expense of everyone else. If you've been left feeling depleted — emotionally, physically, or financially — you may have been exploited and used for their selfish gain. People have used the term energy-drainers, emotional vampires, etc., to refer to such people. While these terms are not scientific, they sure are revealing enough to help us understand DTers better.

At this juncture, it must be clarified that the above details of the Dark Triad attempt to explain the subclinical manifestation of these traits. That is why the Big 5 traits were explored too, because clinical expressions of the Dark Triad do not need such detailed exploration.

The word "clinical" means that the deviant behavior was observable. The term subclinical refers primarily to the extent of a condition wherein the behaviors examined are milder than its clinical version. But, even though the disease does not manifest harshly or vividly enough, it is still vicious enough to cause horrible damage. In fact, the milder versions might be even more dangerous because clinical intensity will be recognized more often, and some treatment might be administered. However, the subclinical manifestation of Dark Triads can be subtle and thus hidden, making it harder to detect and therefore harder to counter.

To illuminate this further, the word clinical refers to a scale where it is an apparent and severe disorder/disease/illness. Subclinical implies less severity and indicates a subtle condition that might be hard to detect. This means that subclinical levels of the DT conditions will allow the DTers to function in society without hindrances that people with clinical levels of a disease usually have to face.

The difficulty in detecting subclinical Dark Triad behaviors has made Dark Psychology both an enigmatic and a misused label. Very few studies have managed to find concrete insights into the Dark Triad and associated outcomes.

While all the science explained above clearly magnifies our ability to identify manipulators and dangerous Dark Triad proponents. Psychology is a science, but the human mind does not always fall neatly into labels and categories.

We must summarize what we have learned in this chapter with this caveat. Disagreeableness, low sensitivity, and a severe lack of conscientiousness are indicators. When these things are coupled with high intelligence, it could prove even more dangerous. However, does this mean that these things will always allow us to detect manipulators? Unfortunately, no.

Earlier, we had talked about a potential unknown personality trait that could explain the similarities of all the Dark Triad traits. This is an area of constant study and speculation. In the interest of learning and helping people, it is necessary to present additional details about the subject.

What is the one thing that all manipulators share, without a shadow of a doubt? This would have to be an immoral or amoral nature. They lack a set of moral principles. This malice is most prevalent in psychopaths, as indicated by their lowest conscientiousness and lack of conscience.

A test of morality, or merely examining the morals of a suspicious character, could thus prove to be the first and finest indicator of that person's nefariousness. Knowing a person's behavior and analyzing it based on the Dirty Dozen questions could prove instrumental in recognizing a manipulator.

Despite all this invaluable knowledge, it is still possible to face defeat at the hands of a hazardous manipulator. It is frustrating. It is infuriating. But becoming more aware does improve your chances of combating this evil. Speaking of malevolence, there is a rare personality type that can rightly be considered the most dangerous of them all. The harder it is to detect an evil person, the more likely they are to succeed in damaging us. This brings us to the "Dark Empath.".

The Dark Empath

Many Dark Triaders show low agreeableness, conscientiousness, and neuroticism. However, there is evidence that some people exhibit Dark Triad traits but are also capable of showing empathy; they can also be extroverted. (*Garis, 2022*)

These people enjoy social interactions and want to be around people, but they do so because they want to manipulate and dominate them for their own selfish interests.

They can control their empathetic response and use it as a weapon. But, to make it worse, these people can also be genuinely empathetic, meaning they can understand and even feel the emotions of others. This is the Dark Empath. (*Heym et al., 2021*)

Dark Empaths are usually not as overtly aggressive as the sociopathic manipulator. Unfortunately, it has also been found that while ordinary DT people can suffer from debilitating issues regarding their well-being, this problem does not exist for Dark Empaths. (*Heym et al., 2021*)

In other words, Dark Empaths are more invulnerable than other Dark Triads. They are also harder to detect. Now one can understand why it is correct to call them the most dangerous manipulators of them all. (*Heym & Sumich, 2022*). Combining our insights into immorality and the information about the Dark Empath personality, let us consider a more recent trend in psychology. This is called the Dark Tetrad.

This is the term given to the set of personality traits where Sadism is added to the Dark Triad. It may be a more accurate and useful term. Sadism is the immoral desire to hurt others for one's pleasure. Hence the Dark Tetrad concept might give us a further understanding of manipulation. (*Heym et al., 2021*)

When combined with empathy, the Dark Tetrad traits result in the most extreme version of a malicious person, the sadistic Dark Empath. It is easy to understand how complex manipulation is and how difficult it is to beat. It is helpful to understand milder forms of coercion in this regard.

Manipulation is the most extreme form of persuasion. It makes sense for us to know about persuasion because we can gain additional insights that might equip us further in our journey against manipulation. Thus, we shall now look at persuasion and the science surrounding it.

References:

American Psychological Association: APA Dictionary: "Machiavellianism."

Bereczkei, T. (2017). Machiavellianism: The Psychology of Manipulation (1st ed.). Routledge. https://doi.org/10.4324/9781315106922

Big 5 Personality Traits. (2022, March 1). Psychology Today; www.psychologytoday.com. https://www.psychologytoday.com/us/basics/big-5-personality-traits

Black, Donald W., and C. Lindon Larson. Bad Boys, Bad Men, Confronting Antisocial Personality Disorder. New York, NY: Oxford University Press, 1999.

Cleckley, H. M. (2016). The Mask of Sanity.

Freedman, M. David. "False prediction of future dangerousness: Error rates and Psychopathy Checklist-Revised." Journal of the American Academy of Psychiatry and Law 29, no. 1 (March, 2001): 89-95.

Garis, M. G. (2022, February 22). Dark Empath Might Be the Most Dangerous Personality Type | Well+Good. The Dark Empath Personality Merges Empathy With Dark Triad Traits—And That Spells Trouble; www.wellandgood.com. https://www.wellandgood.com/dark-empath/

Grann, M., N. Langström, A. Tengström and G. Kullgren. "Psychopathy (PCL-R) predicts violent recidivism among criminal offenders with personality disorders in Sweden." Law and Human Behavior 23, no. 2 (April, 1999): 205-217.

Hare, Robert D. (February 1, 1996). "Psychopathy and Antisocial Personality Disorder: A Case of Diagnostic Confusion". Psychiatric Times. New York City: MJH Associates. 13 (2).

Hare, Robert D. Without Conscience: The Disturbing World of the Psychopaths Among Us. New York, NY: The Guilford Press, 1993.

Hare, Robert D.; Hart, Stephen D.; Harpur, Timothy J. (1991). "Psychopathy and the DSM-IV criteria for antisocial personality disorder". Journal of Abnormal Psychology. 100 (3): 391–8. doi:10.1037/0021-843X.100.3.391

Heym, N., & Sumich, A. (2022, April 4). Psychologists explain the hidden danger of "dark empaths." PsyPost; www.psypost.org. https://www.psypost.org/2022/04/psychologists-explain-the-hidden-danger-of-dark-empaths-62846

Heym, N., Kibowski, F., Bloxsom, C. A. J., Blanchard, A., Harper, A., Wallace, L., Firth, J., & Sumich, A. (2020, July 29). The dark empath: Characterising dark traits in the presence of empathy. Personality and Individual Differences. Retrieved April 14, 2022, from https://www.sciencedirect.com/science/article/abs/pii/S0191886920303615?via%3Dihub

https://www.theatlantic.com/science/archive/2015/09/the-violence-of-empathy/407155/

Patrick, Christopher (2005). Handbook of Psychopathy. Guilford Press. ISBN 978-1-60623-804-2

Paulhus, D. L., & Williams, K. M. (2002, November 19). The Dark Triad of personality: Narcissism, Machiavellianism, and psychopathy. Journal of Research in Personality. Retrieved April 14, 2022, from https://www.sciencedirect.com/science/article/abs/pii/S0092656602005056

Semple, David (2005). The Oxford Handbook of Psychiatry. Oxford, England: Oxford University Press. pp. 448–9. ISBN 978-0-19-852783-1

Skeem, J. L., Polaschek, D. L. L., Patrick, C. J., & Lilienfeld, S. O. (2011). Psychopathic Personality: Bridging the Gap Between Scientific Evidence and Public Policy. Psychological Science in the Public Interest, 12(3), 95–162. https://doi.org/10.1177/1529100611426706

Sussex Publishers. (n.d.). Dark Triad. Psychology Today. Retrieved April 14, 2022, from https://www.psychologytoday.com/us/basics/dark-triad

Sussex Publishers. (n.d.). Openness. Psychology Today. Retrieved April 14, 2022, from https://www.psychologytoday.com/us/basics/openness

Key Chapter Two Takeaways

1. The Dark Triad Personality traits are Machiavellianism, Narcissism, and Psychopathy. They are strong indicators of potential manipulators.

2. The more common manipulators exhibit high levels of Extroversion, low levels of Agreeableness, low levels of Neuroticism, and low levels of Conscientiousness.

3. Of the Dark Triad, Psychopathy is the worst, followed by Machiavellianism.

4. The twelve questions of the Dirty Dozen test are a useful indicator to help detect Dark Triad personalities.

5. Common patterns seen in the lives of Dark Triad people include a history of failed relationships, portraying themselves as false victims, inconsistencies in their stories, and persistent demand for attention.

6. Manipulators all have one thing in common; they lack morals.

7. Dark Tetrad accounts for the Dark Triad along with the trait of sadism.

8. Dark Empaths are the most dangerous personality type because they can be empathetic and thus very hard to detect. In one study, only thirteen percent of the sample population had Dark Triad traits and low empathy. However, twenty percent of the sample exhibited Dark Triad states AND empathy, making them potential Dark Empaths.

9. Due to the complexity of Dark Psychology, it is now optimal to study a less virulent but more prevalent form of influence called Persuasion.

CHAPTER THREE

PERSUASION VS MANIPULATION

Odds are, you've tried to persuade someone to do or think something at some point in your life. People who work in sales or who enjoy debating are two excellent examples of people using persuasion and persuasive tactics. In fact, most of us try to persuade people to do things every day. So does that make us all manipulators?

For the purposes of this book, manipulation and persuasion are two different ways of influencing people. While persuasion does involve trying to convince people to do or think certain things, it is not the same as manipulation because of the harmful intent and outcomes. To summarize:

- The main difference between persuasion and manipulation is often the malicious intent driving manipulation.
- Are the tactics being used meant to help the other person? Or will they only result in a benefit for the person doing the persuading? Worse, will the influencing action actively harm the other person?

Persuasion differs from manipulation in that it often encourages positive benefits and cooperation. Successful persuasion is the art of convincing others to do what you want them to do because they want to, not because they are forced to.

The difference is more apparent now. Manipulators have a clear winner in mind—themselves. It makes no difference to them whether their victim actually wants to do what is being asked of them, and it doesn't matter if their victim feels regret or remorse afterward. Once again, this makes it clear why manipulation is an assault on individual freedom and liberty.

Persuasion is also used in marketing, advertising, and commerce. These are generally sectors of the economy where the public is sensitive to targeted interactions with media and where convincing people is the goal. While even persuasion is used maliciously in these areas, one cannot deny the importance of persuasion.

Imagine a hypothetical situation in which a salesperson wants to sell his merchandise. In addition to being functional, these products must be appealing and, in some way, better than those of the competition. However, even these truths are not enough. The people do not know about the product. (*Siggelkow, 2007*)

The consumer must be aware of the product/s mentioned above and their value. This awareness is often accomplished through persuasion and advertising, engaging customers' attention, and effectively informing them of the product or service.

Now, you may wonder why must one learn about persuasion if it is not Dark Psychology aka manipulation, especially in this book. The answer is that sometimes you can know something better by also knowing what it is not! It is the same here and there is an additional reason too. Persuasion is not manipulation but they sure are related.

Persuasion can create market competitiveness, often resulting in dynamic offer optimization. This optimization may promote the development of sustainable economics where consumers can also be winners because of their purchasing power. Basically, companies will compete against each other through massive persuasion campaigns to gain consumer favor.

Another famously ongoing use of persuasion in a civilized community is in implementing the law in the judiciary. For example, in a trial, the lawyers will attempt to use the mechanisms of the legal system and solid rhetoric to persuade the jury and the judge that they deserve to win because the law is on their side.

The famous social psychologist Robert Cialdini is considered one of the most preeminent scholars of persuasion. In MBA classes, students are taught sales and marketing. Cialdini's Influence theories were considered the Bible of Marketing and Persuasion. Persuasion is also an essential topic of discussion in the Harvard Business Review magazine.

We have decided to incorporate those principles of persuasion in this chapter and elsewhere. Their importance will become even more evident later on.

Persuasion is considered both an art and a science. It requires a careful balance of assertiveness without being aggressive or dismissive. To successfully persuade without manipulation, you need an ethical core and a sense of integrity.

- Persuasion plays a vital role in the social society in which you exist.
- Take a moment and think about the people who try to influence you daily. What about you? Who do you try to persuade?

To effectively distinguish between persuasion and manipulation, it is necessary to grasp the ethics that underpin positive influence. According to some communication theorists, persuasion is ethically neutral. (*The Difference Between Persuasion & Manipulation, 2015*) In other words, persuasion is neither good nor harmful but rather a neutral process.

However, some people do not agree with the statement above. They believe that Aristotle's notion of persuasion is noble rather than neutral is true. Aristotle emphasized that persuasion is fundamentally desirable since it is one of the effective techniques through which truth is discovered. The "father of logic" thought rhetoric (the persuasive part of discourse) was a noble endeavor. We would have to agree.

A concept is presented with facts through ethical persuasion, and a person is free to accept or reject that compelling appeal. In the Harvard Business Review, it was stated that persuasion does require pushing individuals to a stance they don't currently hold. (*Conger, 2010*)

It takes careful planning, the proper structuring of arguments, the presentation of vivid supporting data, and the attempt to discover the appropriate emotional connection with your audience. This is not immoral.

The fact that contemporary economics, counseling techniques, and the legal system are based on the assumption that persuasion is an ethical and successful way of achieving truth, demonstrates that this belief is ubiquitous. Consequently, persuasion can be considered one of the cornerstones of a functioning democracy.

Democracies could engage in intelligent and ethical persuasion, especially when electing political leaders, adopting laws, or attempting to safeguard their population (*The Difference Between Persuasion & Manipulation, 2015*).

Even those who do not like the concept of persuasion cannot easily avoid it. Human speech is rife with persuasion. People actively and inadvertently encourage particular views and habits when they communicate. As a result, dealing with persuasion is not a choice; it is almost inherent in social contact. Moreover, it is so widespread in human communication that it is practically invisible because people have taken it for granted and do not even care to recognize it.

The so-called people professions – politics, law, social work, counseling, corporate management, advertising, sales, public relations, and the ministry – may be called persuasive professions. (*The Difference Between Persuasion & Manipulation, 2015*)

Persuasion can be influence done for the propagation of truth. In addition, positive change can come as a result of persuasion. Let us look at a few examples of how persuasion can be used for positive outcomes.

Persuasive messages have been scientifically demonstrated to encourage high school students to quit smoking, increase vital blood donations, and discourage adolescents from entering gangs. (*Breen & Matusitz, 2009*)

Charity and charitable organizations rely heavily on persuasion to raise funds. Persuasion influences drivers to wear seat belts or refrain from driving after having alcoholic drinks.

Persuasion may be used to convince an alcoholic or drug-addicted family member to obtain professional assistance to quit their addiction. The coach of an underdog team may motivate the players to give their best through persuasion.

Persuasion is a practice that parents often use to encourage their children to do good things and avoid doing the bad, such as not accepting a lift from strangers or allowing anybody to touch their bodies. (*The Difference Between Persuasion & Manipulation, 2015*)

In summary, persuasion lies at the heart of many constructive, prosocial initiatives. Without persuasion, much of the positives in the world today would not exist.

However, it is not the efficacy of persuasion or the fact that it is ingrained in human nature that makes persuasion a cause for concern. The corruption of influence is what is worrying. It is true that when persuasion is twisted, it may turn into manipulation, which is harmful. (*The Difference Between Persuasion & Manipulation, 2015*)

Con artists, cult leaders, and tyrants have tortured, enslaved, and even murdered millions via deception. Even though they are closely related, manipulation should never be mistaken for noble persuasion. Manipulation is a twisted and malignant kind of persuasion. It is more concerned with malice than with the propagation of truth.

In his well-known work, Rhetoric, Aristotle opined that misuse of rhetorical talent could produce immense evil. He felt this was true of all good things, save virtue. Aristotle was entirely correct in his assertion about the potential of rhetoric.

Aristotle asserted that even the most beneficial things, such as strength, health, money, and military ability, could be used for evil. When used morally, they may be the greatest blessing; when used unethically, they can bring terrible harm.

A salesperson who feels that everyone will profit from his goods and that the customer's life would be much better due to the purchase could use positive persuasion if his assertion is true.

A salesman with the opposite mindset is likelier to employ dubious approaches to persuade a customer to buy. He will adopt an "ends justify the means" mentality. Naturally, this exposes the user to questionable sales practices. These practices become harmful when the manipulative salesman's actions directly hurt the consumer. This scenario illustrates the thin line where persuasion gives way to manipulation.

Assessing intention—manipulation or persuasion? If you are unsure whether someone is trying to persuade or manipulate you, consider these questions:

1. What is their goal for this interaction?
2. Who benefits and how?
3. Do I feel good about how they are approaching the interaction? What does my gut say?
4. Are they trying to convince me of something I disagree with?

Now that you know the critical difference between persuasion and manipulation let's look at the six universal principles of persuasion identified by research. There is a huge advantage in learning about the exact science behind persuasion.

Robert Cialdini's work has taught persuasion to many people across the world. This splendid work is excellent for us too. In line with this book's theme, knowledge of the 'enemy' is vital to defeating them.

References:

Aristotle. Rhetoric, (W. Rhys Roberts, Translator). (Mineola, New York: Dover Publications, Inc., 2004). 1355b15.

Crano, W. D., & Prislin, R. (2006). Attitudes and persuasion. Annu. Rev. Psychol., 57, 345-374.

Duncan, R. D. (2018, December 21). Influence Versus Manipulation: Understand The Difference. Forbes; www.forbes.com. https://www.forbes.com/sites/rodgerdeanduncan/2018/12/21/influence-vs-manipulation-understand-the-difference/?sh=73b46f28470c

Fagan, A. (2017, September 5). Weapons of Mass Persuasion | Psychology Today. Psychology Today; www.psychologytoday.com. https://www.psychologytoday.com/us/articles/201709/weapons-mass-persuasion

Franke, M., & Rooij, R. V. (2015). Strategies of persuasion, manipulation and propaganda: Psychological and social aspects. Models of strategic reasoning, 255-291.

G.Breen and J. Matusitz. "Preventing yours from join gangs: How to apply inoculation theory." Journal of Applied Security Research, 4, 2009. p. 109 – 128.

Gallo, C. (2019, July 15). The Art of Persuasion Hasn't Changed in 2,000 Years. Harvard Business Review; hbr.org. https://hbr.org/2019/07/the-art-of-persuasion-hasnt-changed-in-2000-years

Jay Conger. "The Necessary Art of Persuasion." Harvard Business Review Onpoint, Fall 2010. p. 46.

Nagaraj, V., & Frey, J. (2021, February 25). The Ethical Edge of Persuasion. Psychology Today; www.psychologytoday.com. https://www.psychologytoday.com/us/blog/leading-in-the-real-world/202102/the-ethical-edge-persuasion

Persuasion. (2022, March 1). Psychology Today; www.psychologytoday.com. https://www.psychologytoday.com/us/basics/persuasion

Siggelkow, N. (2007). Persuasion with case studies. Academy of management journal, 50(1), 20-24.

Taillard, M., Giscoppa, H. (2013). Organizational Manipulation. In: Psychology and Modern Warfare. Palgrave Macmillan, New York. https://doi.org/10.1057/9781137347329_20

The Difference Between Persuasion & Manipulation | Hoffeld Group. (2015, April 28). Hoffeld Group; www.hoffeldgroup.com. https://www.hoffeldgroup.com/the-difference-between-persuasion-manipulation/

The Difference Between Persuasion & Manipulation. (2015, April 28). Hoffeld Group; www.hoffeldgroup.com. https://www.hoffeldgroup.com/the-difference-between-persuasion-manipulation/

Key Chapter Takeaways

1. Persuasion is a form of influence that has led to many positive outcomes.

2. Persuasion can be positive if used to inform people about their options; people are then free to make a choice.

3. The tools of persuasion have been corrupted by manipulators and used for manipulation instead of noble persuasion.

4. Persuasion often makes use of the language tool known as rhetoric. Rhetoric is the use of words to persuade others.

5. Persuasion is a core concept in the functioning of democracies. Government and government initiatives can work through persuasion.

6. Try to differentiate between persuasion and manipulation by considering the situation through questions such as the goals of an interaction, who are its beneficiaries, what you feel about the outcome, and whether it agrees with your principles.

CHAPTER FOUR

PRINCIPLES OF PERSUASION

Persuasion is most effective when it appeals to specific deep-rooted human responses and impulses. Social psychologists have identified these through high-quality research and experimentation. These impulses can be considered part of the human condition, which should also tell us that it is possible to be immune to it. The responses can also be neatly categorized into six principles, which you will learn in this chapter.

These Principles of Persuasion are part of the ground-breaking work by Dr. Robert B. Cialdini, a renowned social psychologist and academic from the United States. His work describes each principle and the reasoning for its inclusion on the list. Dr. Cialdini's work has been studied in academia and corporate offices for several decades and has stood the test of time.

Influence: The Psychology of Persuasion is Cialdini's most well-known work. It was built on three years of working "undercover" at used car dealerships, fund-raising groups, and telemarketing corporations to study real-life persuasive scenarios. (*Cialdini, 2009*)

Dr. Robert Cialdini has studied what motivates individuals to say yes to specific sales requests. His study findings, subsequent publications, and New York Times bestseller books have given him a prestigious reputation as a renowned scientist in the field of persuasion. His writings, including Influence and Persuasion, have sold over seven million copies in forty-four languages.

He is widely regarded as the world's foremost authority on the science of persuasion and how it should be used in business. His Principles of Persuasion have become a cornerstone for every company concerned with successfully enhancing its influence.

This backstory is meant to cement the fact that what follows in this chapter is vital in illuminating dark psychology. We have determined that even persuasion can be corrupted, and the tools of persuasion can easily be used as manipulation devices. Ergo, it is clear that we must become familiar with these tools.

To better comprehend the principles of persuasion, we must first learn how persuasion might affect the mind. This need requires us to become familiar with certain terms and concepts often used in the study of persuasion.

We will thus consider the major aspects of the persuasion process: the originating source, the receiver, and the message itself. (*Siggelkow, 2007*)

Issuer

When it comes to who transfers the information (the persuader who is trying to convince), two criteria are considered significant in determining the success of the persuasion: their attractiveness and credibility.

Multiple tests have demonstrated that we typically regard those we view as credible also to be dependable (partly due to the halo effect, in which we presume that someone with one positive attribute would inevitably have others). Unfortunately, this effect also seems to apply to attractive people.

This affinity for attractiveness is why men and women of exceptional physical appeal and well-known celebrities commonly feature in advertisements to sell us various products. (*Siggelkow, 2007*)

However, when it comes to convincing people, the more powerful aspect of the source is his/her credibility. In this context, the source's credibility is defined as their level of skill in the subject area and their perceived sincerity. Credibility has the potential to persuade more intelligent people where mere celebrity status would not prevail.

This credibility is why arguments from authority sources are so compelling to many people. It is also why someone considered intelligent carries a lot of clout when it comes to perceived reliability.

Receiver

Regarding the message's recipient, the primary criteria that impact the time, possibility, and scale of being affected, are intellect, self-esteem, and engagement with the issue.

Intelligence typically refers to the ability to acquire and process information efficiently. People who have this skill tend to obtain significant influence in their circles. On the flip side, they also tend to be more immune to the persuasive attempts of others. This protection is because those who are more intelligent tend to have more resources to evaluate the persuasion they are being subjected to. (*Siggelkow, 2007*)

Since more intelligent individuals have a greater capacity to absorb and use the knowledge they have learned in real-time, their conversation style is more fluid and consistent. This skill is reflected in the behavioral outcomes of persuasion.

It is undeniably harder to persuade more intelligent people. Usually, the success of the persuasion attempt will depend on whether the receiver desires the potential outcome of the call-to-action enough to proceed.

In terms of self-esteem, typically, the lower someone's self-esteem, the less likely they are to believe their own arguments, and the more they prefer accepting the opinions of others. Also, the more a person is exposed to the influence process, the more likely it is that the persuasion will succeed.

Summing up, two factors determining the eventual success of most attempts at persuasion are the receiver's intelligence and the amount of time the receiver is exposed to the persuasion action. This knowledge is going to be exceedingly valuable.

Message

When it comes to influencing someone, it is evident that one of the most important factors is the message itself. Several studies show that using a more rational or emotional message depends on the reaction you wish to elicit. (*Siggelkow, 2007*). Either way, Pathos, and Logos are established parts of Rhetoric. They stand for appeals to emotion and logical reasoning, respectively.

It is sometimes better to use open-ended messages to make the persuasive action likelier to succeed. Even if the entire communication was designed to steer the recipient/s in the persuader's chosen direction, open-ended statements could give the receiver the impression that they chose the action themselves.

This difference is significant because listeners feel more satisfied when they reach such conclusions in this manner, feeling as if they made the discovery themselves. People would prefer that instead of someone attempting to impose an idea on them. (*Siggelkow, 2007*)

Now that we know about the three elements of the persuasion process, let us dive into the six principles of persuasion that will illustrate the tactics commonly used.

The Six Principles of Persuasion

1. Reciprocity

People often feel obligated to return what they have received as a gift or a free service. For example, if a friend invites you to a party, you would most likely feel that you owe it to them to ask them to a forthcoming party you are holding.

If a colleague does you a favor, you may believe you are indebted to that friend and owe them a favor in return. As a result, most people are more inclined to say yes to individuals they feel obligated to.

Suppose a non-profit organization sends someone a pen in exchange for completing a standard donation form. In that case, this significantly improves the chance of another donation because of the sense of obligation created.

A sales expert can deliver several minor services to a customer, making the latter feel obliged to buy something. In the earlier chapter on manipulation, we explained how fear, obligation, and guilt were common emotional responses targeted by manipulators.

Accordingly, you can now see more clearly how obligation can be used for both persuasion and manipulation. This sense of debt is a foundational feature of the human condition.

When prehistoric humans transitioned from solitary hunters to living in a tribe, they discovered that this community-living entailed wanting to perform something beneficial for others to obtain an obligatory response after a while. Words like favor, debt, honor, obligation, etc., are used to describe this process.

The principle of reciprocity arose as a result of this. One of the most important takeaways of this principle is that reciprocity worked even when the initial favor was not requested. The only thing that seems to matter is that the persuading party offered a gift before the persuasion action.

Even if the recipient had not demanded the offered gift, and even if they did not eventually accept the present, the recipient still felt obligated by the gesture. This condition sounds very similar to the phrase, "it is the thought that counts".

2. Scarcity

People want things they cannot live without. They also like items that they do not have. But they often also desire things that seem rare and uncommon. This rarity is called scarcity, and it leads to potential exclusivity.

Exclusivity creates desire because people want to feel special and unique, and owning exclusive things is one way to achieve it.

When British Airways declared in 2003 that it would no longer operate the twice-daily London—New York Concorde trip because it had become unprofitable, sales skyrocketed the next day.

No changes were made to the Concorde itself. It did not fly any faster, the service did not improve, and the ticket price did not fall. The declaration about its ending made the Concorde appear as a limited resource. As a result, the people desired it even more.

So, when it comes to effectively influencing people, one must consider utilizing the Scarcity Principle. It's not enough to merely tell folks about the advantages of using your goods and services.

You'll also need to highlight what makes your idea distinctive and what they stand to lose if they don't consider it. Scarcity often causes higher value perception, even if it is unwarranted. It is more of an emotional reaction.

3. Principle of authority

This principle is based on the notion that people will follow the advice of respectable and informed experts. We have already discussed the influence that authority figures have. This precept works along the same lines.

For example, more patients will follow the professional advice of their physiotherapists if their medical certificates are displayed on the walls of their consulting rooms.

People are more willing to offer change for a ticket machine to a total stranger if the requester is dressed formally rather than casually. Thus, a trivial issue such as someone's clothes can affect perceived authority for many people.

The research tells us that it's essential to indicate to people what makes you a trustworthy, competent authority before attempting to persuade them. But, of course, this might cause issues: You can't go about telling potential clients how great you are, though you can hire someone to do it for you.

Surprisingly, evidence suggests that it doesn't matter if the person praising the persuader's authority is related to them. Inexplicably, even if the person talking about the persuader's authority was benefiting from the introduction, that didn't seem to diminish the effect of the praise. For example, people were more likely to trust a physician if the doctor's secretary mentioned their qualifications to the prospective patient. (*Cialdini, 2004*) Ethos/appeals to authority were identified as powerful rhetorical devices more than 2,000 years ago in Ancient Greece.

Like the above example of doctors, real estate agents have improved their property evaluations and subsequent contracts by arranging for trained receptionists. These receptionists who handle consumer inquiries were asked to emphasize their colleagues' credentials and experience.

In the case of one particular firm, customers who wanted to rent a property were informed, "Lettings? Let me put you in touch with Deborah, who has been renting out apartments in this region for over fifteen years. " Customers who wished to sell their homes were urged to "speak to Peter, our head of sales. He has been selling real estate for nearly twenty years. I'll put you through right now."

The impact of this professional introduction resulted in a twenty percent increase in the number of hires and a fifteen percent rise in the number of contracts signed. That is not bad for a minor tweak that was neither immoral nor untrue.

4. Consistency and commitment

People like to stick to what they have already said or done. This behavior is a founding principle behind the psychology of habits.

Consistency is triggered by seeking tiny first commitments. In a renowned series of experiments, researchers unexpectedly discovered that relatively few individuals would be prepared to put an unattractive wooden board on their front yard to promote a Drive Safely campaign in their community. The value of the message was immaterial to the owners.

However, four times as many residents in a nearby identical community said they would be prepared to put up this awful billboard. Why? Because ten days previously, they had agreed to put a little postcard in their front windows to express their support for a Drive Safely campaign. (*Cialdini, 2004*)

That modest card was the starting point for the persuasion. Here the people had gotten used to spreading the Drive Safely message using an agreeably small-sized message on space they owned. Hence, they did not resist the demand when asked to put the much bigger wooden board and even wholeheartedly supported the venture.

The consistency and commitment principles can work together. Here, the instigator of the persuasion looks for free, active, and public commitments and ideally should obtain those promises in writing. This action is done because people seem more receptive to doing things they agreed to do in writing. The people felt compelled to act upon what they claimed simply because they had physically written it down.

For example, a recent study found that merely getting patients to write details about future appointments on appointment cards reduced nonappearances at health facilities by eighteen percent.

5. Liking

People are more likely to say yes to people they like. But what is it that makes one individual like another? According to persuasion science, there are three critical variables. We enjoy the company of individuals who are like us, people who compliment us, and those who work with us to achieve shared goals.

As more and more of our contacts take place online, it's worth considering if these elements can be used effectively in online negotiations.

In a series of negotiation experiments conducted between MBA students at two renowned business schools, some groups were taught that "time is money. " Another motto used was, "Let's get down to business. " Around fifty-five percent of those in this group could reach an agreement.

However, a second group was told, "Before you start bargaining, discuss some personal details with one other. Then, find a point of commonality between you and start bargaining." In this group, ninety percent reached effective and agreeable outcomes that were generally worth eighteen percent more to both sides.

As explained before, people are also inclined to like attractive people.

6. Social proof

People will look to the actions and behaviors of others to define their own, especially when people are uncertain of their abilities and choices.

You may have observed that some hotels frequently leave a tiny card in restrooms to try and encourage visitors to reuse their towels and sheets. Most do this by attracting visitors' attention to the environmental benefits of reuse. (*Cialdini, 2017*). It turns out that this is a moderately effective method, resulting in around thirty-five percent compliance. Is there, however, a more effective way?

It turns out that more than seventy-five percent of customers who stay in a hotel for four nights or longer reuse their towels at some point. So, taking a cue from the Principle of Social Proof, what if one just placed that information on the cards and said that seventy-five percent of visitors reuse their towels at some point during their stay, so please do the same? When they did this, towel reuse increased further by twenty-six percent.

Imagine seeing one of these signs the next time you stay in a hotel. When you picked it up, you saw the following message: "75% of guests who have been in this room have reused their towel." What are your thoughts? So, you could think, "I hope they're not the same towels." And, like most individuals, you probably believe this sign will not affect your conduct.

However, it turns out that modifying only a few words on a sign to state what comparable past visitors did was a compelling message, resulting in a thirty-three percent boost in reuse. The research tells us that rather than depending on one's capacity to convince others, the persuader may instead refer to what others similar to the consumer in question are currently doing.

Social proof is the backbone of the digital business world. The number of likes, dislikes, comments, posts, etc., determines what is "viral" precisely because people look for what others have liked and disliked.

Facebook, Amazon, Google, YouTube, and many other organizations work through reviews, likes, views, and clicks because these are the digital equivalent of a positive testimonial or reference. As a result, people tend to trust a product or service more, if a large group has liked it.

For decades, corporations and marketers have utilized these six principles of influence to persuade you, the customer, to spend as much money as possible.

Having discussed the science of persuasion, one can see clearly that the techniques of persuasion closely match those of manipulation. This resemblance is because the underlying principle behind these techniques is often the same.

We can now move into more detailed types of inter-personal manipulation. Let us begin by looking at a widespread, overt, and storied type of devious psychological manipulation that is criminal and heinous—the confidence trick, also known as conning.

References:

Berinato, S. (2019, January 0). Data Science and the Art of Persuasion. Harvard Business Review; hbr.org. https://hbr.org/2019/01/data-science-and-the-art-of-persuasion

Cialdini, R. (2017). Pre-Suasion. Random House Business Books.

Cialdini, R. B. (2001, October 1). Harnessing the Science of Persuasion. Harvard Business Review; hbr.org. https://hbr.org/2001/10/harnessing-the-science-of-persuasion

Cialdini, R. B. (2007). Influence. https://doi.org/10.1604/9780061241895

Cialdini, R. B. (2013, July 1). The Uses (and Abuses) of Influence. Harvard Business Review; hbr.org. https://hbr.org/2013/07/the-uses-and-abuses-of-influence

Cialdini, R. B., & Goldstein, N. J. (2004). Social influence: Compliance and conformity. Annu. Rev. Psychol., 55, 591-621.

Huang, L., & Yu, R. (2020, July 31). How to (Actually) Change Someone's Mind. Harvard Business Review; hbr.org. https://hbr.org/2020/07/how-to-actually-change-someones-mind

Knight, R. (2017, May 22). How to Improve Your Sales Skills, Even If You're Not a Salesperson. Harvard Business Review; hbr.org. https://hbr.org/2017/05/how-to-improve-your-sales-skills-even-if-youre-not-a-salesperson

Ross, J. (2009, March 17). Three Ways to Be More Persuasive. Harvard Business Review; hbr.org. https://hbr.org/2009/03/three-ways-to-be-more-persuasi

Siggelkow, N. (2007). Persuasion with case studies. Academy of management journal, 50(1), 20-24.

Teeny, J.D., Siev, J.J., Briñol, P., & Petty, R. E. (2021). A review and conceptual framework for understanding personalized matching effects in persuasion. Journal of Consumer Psychology. DOI: 10.1002/jcpy.1198

Update, H. M. (2008, February 27). The Language of Persuasion. Harvard Business Review; hbr.org. https://hbr.org/2008/02/the-language-of-persuasion

Key Chapter Four Takeaways

1. With Persuasion, the issuer/persuader is more likely to succeed if they are attractive or credible. Credibility is a more powerful driver than attractiveness.

2. Regarding the recipient of the persuasive action, the more intelligent they are, the harder it is to persuade them unless they wish for the outcome of the persuasive action. Additionally, the more time the receiver is exposed to persuasion, the more likely they agree.

3. Concerning the actual message of the persuasion, the more powerful the emotional appeal and the more weighty the rational and logical strength of the persuasive action, the more likely it is to succeed.

4. Reciprocity is the First Principle of Persuasion. People who feel obligated to the persuader are far more likely to be persuaded.

5. Scarcity is a strong persuasion device. People crave limited resources that seem rare and cherish exclusivity because it makes them feel unique and special.

6. Authority is often used for persuasion. Persuaders who appear to be reliable and credible sources of authority tend to experience greater success in persuasion.

7. People are more likely to be persuaded if they have done something similar to the requested action. They are also more likely to perform something for which they have given a written commitment.

8. Folks are more likely to say yes to people they like. This liking can stem from familiarity, flattery, and cooperation.

9. Social proof is one of the most potent forms of persuasion. Most people tend to like or dislike things based on what others say.

PART II

"MANO E MANO"
INTERPERSONAL MANIPULATION

CHAPTER FIVE

THE COVERT CONFIDENCE TRICK

This chapter explains a confidence trick and the various stages of a "confidence game". Whether or not you know it, you've likely heard of confidence tricks. These are the classic cons you think of when you think of general manipulation and deception. They include card tricks, rigged games, insurance fraud, investment scams, and others you might not be familiar with.

The Oxford Languages Dictionary defines a confidence trick or confidence game as "a swindle in which the victim is first persuaded to trust the swindler in some way before the victim is tricked." Among professional con men, the human vulnerabilities commonly exploited are dishonesty, greed, and the gullibility of the marks (targets).

Frauds and scams are heinous crimes that destroy people's lives and shatter their futures. The repercussions of such vile thefts can be felt for several generations. Among the reported crimes, Americans lost 5.8 Billion dollars to fraud in 2021 alone. This number was higher than the 2020 figure of 3.4 Billion dollars. These are the official statistics from The Federal Trade Commission. (*Iacurci, 2022*)

The unofficial stats estimation is that Americans have lost up to 30 billion dollars to phone-based scams alone. Up to 1 in 3 Americans report being scammed through the phone. Truecaller reports claim that roughly 60 million Americans have lost money to phone scams. (*Leonhardt, 2021*)

Identity theft and credit card fraud are other massive sectors where rotten criminals victimize innocent people. Nearly 5 million identity theft and credit card fraud reports were made to the Federal Trade Commission in 2020 alone. The monetary loss amounted to 4.5 billion dollars. Once again, this was a 45%

increase from 2019. Hence the trend is crystal clear. Such crimes are constantly increasing. (*Schulte, 2022*) And fraud is not just an American problem either.

In India, it is estimated that there is 1 billion (100 crores) rupees worth of bank frauds happening every single day! (*Kumar, 2022*)

According to Scamwatch, Australians lost a record 211 million dollars to scams in 2021, an 89% increase from 2020 scam losses. (*Losses Reported to Scamwatch Exceed $211 Million, Phone Scams Exploding | ACCC, 2021*)

In this chapter, we will learn about the various patterns found in confidence scams. Familiarity leads to awareness and this, in turn, provides a measure of protection on its own. But, first, let us look at the backdrop of this manipulation scheme.

Con, trust game, confidence plan, swindle, scam, etc., are all synonyms of the same kind of criminal behavior. A confidence trick perpetrator is also known as a confidence man, con-artist, or "grifter." The shell game or the short-con is an old form of a confidence trick that can be traced back to Ancient Greece.

One of the first confidence men of the modern era was Samuel Thompson (1821–1856). Thompson was a sloppy con artist who encouraged his victims to show their trust in him by handing him money or their wristwatch rather than demonstrating their confidence more subtly. Unfortunately, a few unsuspecting people did put their money and watches in Thompson's hands. Thompson was apprehended in July of 1849.

When reporting on the arrest, James Houston, a journalist for the New York Herald, dubbed Thompson the "Confidence Man." Although Thompson was a failed fraudster, he earned a false reputation as a brilliant operator mainly because people misunderstood Houston's humorous and sarcastic tone.

This incorrect comprehension led to the phrase becoming a part of the lexicon for the wrong reasons. (Similar mistakes include the widespread incorrect use of terms such as "American Indians, " "Asian-Americans, " and so forth.)

The origin of the label "the confidence trick" is not nearly as significant as the severe weakness that was exploited by that first low-skilled 'confidence' trickster: the gullibility of the victims. Gullibility is typically a sign of low intelligence.

Let us now look at the usual process behind the confidence trick.

The stages

The Big Con is often a finely choreographed play with six acts, each with its own particular role in bringing the mark closer to the eventual conclusion when his wealth will be snatched away. Even the target has his lines, and just because he doesn't know them, it doesn't mean he won't tell the con-man when the time is perfect.

The mark will unknowingly tell the scammer everything necessary for the con to work. Even the dialogue is usually structured so that the mark's replies are the most predictable things he will say, given the circumstance. (*Maurer & Sante, 1999*)

David Maurer, a mid-twentieth-century academic linguist, was fascinated with criminal jargon. Accordingly, he conducted a considerable study (*Maurer & Sante, 1999*) of swindlers and grifters, decoding their language while studying their sociology. As a result, he developed the stages of a big con as follows.

Foundation work

Preparation for the game includes recruiting any necessary assistance and researching the required background information. Unfortunately, with advanced digital technologies, scammers have found new ways to discover things about their potential marks.

Approach

The victim is contacted or approached. It has been seen that the approach is often designed to immediately make the trickster as likable to the mark as possible. Interestingly, many of the tools of persuasion and manipulation discussed earlier are used in this regard.

These criminals often appear credible, authoritative, attractive, etc.

Build-up

The victim is allowed to benefit by taking part in a program. In this situation, the criminal targets the victim's greed, and the victim's view of the circumstances may be distorted. As mentioned, dishonesty, greed, and gullibility are the typical targets of conmen.

I spoke to a friend of mine recently who talked about her career as a serial entrepreneur. Coincidentally, she also mentioned the innumerable scammers who target entrepreneurs specifically due to their inherent risk-taking mentality and typically greater wealth.

Pay-off or 'Convincer'

The victim receives a small reward as proof of the scheme's alleged efficacy. This might be real money, or it could be a false payment in some way. A gambling con allows the victim to win multiple little wagers. The victim of a stock market fraud is paid phony dividends.

It is pretty easy to understand that this tactic is often the most significant factor in convincing the mark. This false reward tends to shatter the reservations of many marks. These victims then constantly place excessive trust in their predators.

The "hurrah"

A sudden fabricated crisis or shift in events drives the victim to act or make a choice immediately. This stage is the point where the con either succeeds or fails. For example, in financial fraud, the con artist may inform the victim that the "big opportunity" to make a substantial investment in the plan will close abruptly and permanently.

One can note the similarity between this and the "Scarcity" Principle in Persuasion. They both work on the creation of false urgency. Scarcity creates false urgency; in this case, the urgency is created by the notion of "FOMO" (Fear of Missing Out).

The in-and-in

A conspirator (who is in on the con but seems to be an interested bystander) invests money in the same plan as the victim to provide credibility. This additional input can comfort the victim while giving the con-man more power after the sale is complete. This part is analogous to the Social Proof principle of persuasion.

Gluttony, dishonesty, vanity, opportunism, desire, sympathy, credulity, irresponsibility, despair, and naivety are all used in confidence tricks. As a result, there is no regular profile of a confidence-trick target (also known as a mark). Instead, the common aspect is that a con-victim often relies on the con-man's good faith.

Victims of scams tend to be greedy and/or gullible, and many con artists frequently target the aged and other vulnerable people, employing different confidence tactics. In addition, researchers Huang and Orbach have found that con-men are successful in causing mistakes in judgment. This error is usually a result of misinformation and cognitive biases.

These errors are created when the human faculty for reason is trumped by the marks' dishonesty, greed, and/or gullibility. There is a saying that one cannot cheat an honest guy. This concept is not literally true, but it references the fact that the mark's readiness to participate in immoral behaviors to make a 'quick buck' is often the reason for their downfall.

Similarly, the greed that drives some people to try and get something for nothing and get too-good-to-be-true profits results in marks being taken for a ride.

Many gullible people are sometimes dishonest and greedy, too, almost implying that it takes higher intelligence to be prudently honest and not greedy. A large group of naive people, regarded as "deserving prey" by many, are found typically engaging in injudicious voluntary transactions. (*Huang et al., 2018*) Think of the famous proverb, a fool and his money are soon parted.

We have explored the big con. It is the most well-known method. However, because of this fact, many new conmen have resorted to more psychological and, thus, high-functioning forms of subtle manipulation. This progression is natural as Maurer's work was written many decades ago. The principles might remain the same, but the details will definitely have changed.

Given this book's purpose, let us look at the most common methods of psychological persuasion used by confidence men. (I recommend looking for patterns and similarities in these methods, especially those that remind you of the theoretical concepts we have already gone through in earlier chapters.)

Mere exposure effect

The psychological phenomenon known as the mere-exposure effect occurs when people develop a preference for something only because they are familiar with it. (Consider "Consistency" in Cialdini's principles.) This effect is known as the familiarity principle in social psychology.

Words, Chinese characters, photographs of people, paintings, noises, and geometric shapes, have all been used to demonstrate this effect. According to the research on interpersonal attraction, the more frequently someone sees a person, there is a greater chance that the more attractive and likable that person will appear to that someone.

Foot in the door technique

We have already discussed the principle behind this method earlier. It works like Cialdini's consistency principle. This technique starts with asking someone for something small. If they agree and comply with the small request, they will usually respond positively to the subsequent more significant request.

Remember the earlier example of an ugly wooden board on the property when a small message card to Drive Safely had already been placed in the window? That is a perfect example of this principle.

Door-in-the-face technique

We have explored this principle as well. This works on the obligation->guilt process. The door-in-the-face approach is a compliance strategy. The persuader tries to coerce the target to agree by first making a ludicrous-sounding request that the participant will almost certainly refuse. What follows the rejection will be the actual request.

This strategy achieves compliance by increasing the victim's chance to agree to a subsequent minor request by first asking for something bigger. You start making a large request that a person is likely to deny. Then you make a smaller request that the person finds hard to refuse because most people believe they should not always say no.

Cons come in various forms that are continually evolving. However, all cons rely on two crucial elements: gaining the mark's trust—the reason why the schemes are still known as "confidence games"—and the bait— an enticing reward that both attracts and disarms the mark. (*Huang et al., 2018*)

Before proceeding further to the case study section, I find it helpful to look at typical examples of confidence scams.

Examples of confidence games

- **Get-rich-quick schemes**

Examples of this tactic are products and services that provide implausible wealth in return for tiny payments. This is the most basic form of the confidence trick, and it is shocking how millions of people still fall for such schemes after all these decades of study and exposure. Even more incredible is that people who have fallen for this before still fall victims to new conning schemes. This scenario could be analogous to the gambler who keeps losing and still keeps on gambling in the foolish hope that their fortunes will change, allowing them to recuperate their losses.

- **Gold-brick scams**

These are sales of tangible goods for far more than their actual value. Unfortunately, this is a widespread scam in the consumer goods industry. Millions of people fall for this every year.

- **Gold digging and romance scams**

Personal interactions aimed at gaining the target's affection to obtain the target's money are some of the oldest tricks in human history. Unfortunately, people still succumb to this type of deviousness. It is connected to the oldest "profession" in the world.

- **Humbuggery**

This method is a more advanced tactic that uses controversial public messages to pique public interest and generate a readiness to pay for provocations, amusement, and illusions. Humbuggery may sound infantile, but its potency and prevalence cannot be denied. It is utilized by many different entities, which we will explore later. Artifice is a suitable synonym for humbuggery in this context because the latter shouldn't be considered rubbish.

- **Payoff, rag, and wire schemes**

This refers to ploys that recruit marks to engage in illegal activities such as fixed gambling, insider trading, and embezzlement that are rigged against the marks. These ploys are setups where the trapped mark can never succeed. It is almost like the casino where the "House" will never lose no matter who the gambler is. The key here is the Process that has been set up to bypass the mark's suspicion and scrutiny.

- **Peter Funk**

It is a word describing a phony auctioneer who artificially inflates auction prices. This principle is similar to gold-brick scams explained above: typical work of a swindler.

- **Ponzi schemes**

Perhaps the most famous scam method out there, Ponzi schemes are investment frauds that offer safe or very high returns. They employ deposits to compensate consumers who want to redeem their investments or cash out their earnings. At its simplest, Ponzi schemes are frauds where investors are tricked, and profits are paid to early investors from wealth acquired from recent investors.

This might seem so obvious to fail, and many people wonder how the con-man can make a profit with this. But remember that the late Bernie Madoff, who died aged 82 in 2021 while in prison, had fraudulently scammed 65 billion dollars in what is now known as the largest Ponzi scheme in history.

- **Pyramid and multi-level marketing schemes**

Business concepts that entice participants by promising incentives in exchange for registering others in the program are another form of confidence scam. This kind of scam has seen global traction, and millions of people have fallen victim to it.

But to be honest, it must be said that there have been beneficiaries who managed to become wealthy without incurring losses in this type of scam. However, such instances are far too rare. This is regarded as a scam because people are often not told precisely what the scheme entails.

These and other scams are common across the economy, perpetrated by underworld swindlers, marketers, salespeople, corporations, and politicians. P. T. Barnum, industrial giant Ivar Krueger, Wall Street banker Bernard Madoff, and blood-testing firm founder Elizabeth Holmes are high-profile people who ran large-scale frauds.

As explained earlier, many cons succeed by causing judgment mistakes, most notably errors caused by incomplete information and cognitive biases. As explained earlier, the human weaknesses that cons exploit the most are the marks' dishonesty, greed, and gullibility.

The stories of these confidence tricksters can be read elsewhere. That is not the purpose of this book. Infamous conman Frank Abagnale ended up helping law enforcement learn about confidence scams after he was captured. This proved quite helpful, just like Maurer's undercover work. In line with this book's overarching message, we shall focus on information useful for defeating confidence scams.

The essence of this chapter can now be explored with the help of an anecdote. In India, during the 1970s and 1980s, there lived a man named Mithilesh Kumar Shrivastava. He had a pseudonym, "Natwarlal". He was infamous for having "sold" iconic public buildings like the Taj Mahal, The Red Fort, The Rashtrapathi Bhavan (House of the Indian President), and the Indian Parliament House (Like Capitol Hill) to the wealthy, who were also gullible.

He was eventually apprehended, and when he was brought into court, the judge apparently asked him how he managed to dupe so many people. Natwarlal responded to the judge that he charges a fee of 100 rupees to train pupils with this knowledge of his. The judge supposedly paid Natwarlal the 100 rupees, after which the conman replied that this was his method. (*Bhaduri, 2016*)

The anecdote may be just a story, but its lesson is true. The most commonly used device to con people is the manipulation of emotional desire by countering the mark's better judgment and offering them false wish-fulfillment.

The last part of this chapter will be about the confession of another notorious conman, Victor Lustig. Lustig is widely regarded as one of the most infamous con artists of his time. He is best known as "the man who sold the Eiffel Tower twice" and the perpetrator of the "Rumanian Box" scam. A list of "Ten Commandments for Con-men" has been credited to Lustig. They are incredibly insightful for ordinary, law-abiding, moral people.

- **Be a good listener (this, not fast-talking, gets the results the conman is looking for).**
- **Never appear bored.**
- **Wait for the other person to express any political views before agreeing with them.**
- **Let the other person reveal religious views, then profess to have the same ones.**
- **Hint at romance talk, but don't follow it up unless the other person expresses a strong interest.**
- **Never discuss illness unless some particular concern is shown.**
- **Never inquire about a person's circumstances (they'll eventually tell you everything).**
- **Never brag about your importance; let it be known quietly.**
- **Never be disorganized.**
- **Never, ever get drunk.**

With these ten commandments, this chapter is closed. Confidence scams primarily target wealth and assets. However, manipulation can also occur where intimacy is concerned. In the next chapter, we'll look at a type of manipulation that is more common in close interpersonal relationships.

References:

Bhaduri, A. (2016, February 6). The Confidence Game – Maria Konnikova. Times of India Blog; timesofindia.indiatimes.com. https://timesofindia.indiatimes.com/blogs/just-like-that/the-confidence-game-maria-konnikova/

Bhattacharjee, Y. (2013). The mind of a con man. The New York Times, 28.

DK, Scott, C. (2017). The Crime Book: Big Ideas Simply Explained. London, England: DK Books

FitzGerald, M. (2010, August 1). A Confidence Trick? OUP Academic; academic.oup.com. https://academic.oup.com/policing/article-abstract/4/3/298/1469462

Foster, C. (2014, January 1). Confidence Trick: The Interpretation of Confidence Intervals - Canadian Journal of Science, Mathematics and Technology Education. SpringerLink; link.springer.com. https://link.springer.com/article/10.1080/14926156.2014.874615

Frank Abagnale - Book, Movie & Wife - Biography. (2014, September 2). Biography; www.biography.com. https://www.biography.com/personality/frank-abagnale

Henriques, D. B. (2018). A case study of a con man: Bernie Madoff and the timeless lessons of history's biggest Ponzi scheme. Social Research: An International Quarterly, 85(4), 745-766.

Iacurci, G. (2022, February 22). Consumers lost $5.8 billion to fraud last year — up 70% over 2020. CNBC; www.cnbc.com. https://www.cnbc.com/2022/02/22/consumers-lost-5point8-billion-to-fraud-last-year-up-70percent-over-2020.html

Keen, S., The confidence trick, Australasian Accounting, Business and Finance Journal, 3(1), 2009.

Kumar, C. (2022, March 29). Banking Fraud: India loses Rs 100 crore to banking fraud every day | India Business News - Times of India. The Times of India; timesofindia.indiatimes.com. https://timesofindia.indiatimes.com/business/india-business/india-loses-rs-100-crore-to-banking-fraud-every-day/articleshow/90509071.cms

Leonhardt, M. (2021, June 29). Americans lost $29.8 billion to phone scams over the past year. CNBC; www.cnbc.com. https://www.cnbc.com/2021/06/29/americans-lost-billions-of-dollars-to-phone-scams-over-the-past-year.html

Lindskoog, K., & Wynne, P. (1993). Fakes, Frauds and Other Malarkey. https://doi.org/10.1604/9780310577317

Losses reported to Scamwatch exceed $211 million, phone scams exploding | ACCC. (2021, September 26). Australian Competition and Consumer Commission; www.accc.gov.au. https://www.accc.gov.au/media-release/losses-reported-to-scamwatch-exceed-211-million-phone-scams-exploding

Magazine, S. (2016, March 9). The man who sold the Eiffel Tower. Twice. Smithsonian.com. Retrieved April 14, 2022, from https://www.smithsonianmag.com/history/man-who-sold-eiffel-tower-twice-180958370/

Maurer, D., & Sante, L. (1999). The Big Con. Anchor. https://doi.org/10.1604/9780385495387

Nash, R. M. (2013). Trusting the con man: The role of social networks in the diffusion of fraud (Doctoral dissertation, Arts & Social Sciences: School of Criminology).

Orbach, B., & Huang, L. (2018). Con men and their enablers: The anatomy of confidence games. Social Research: An International Quarterly, 85(4), 795-82

Scott, C. (2019, September 26). The Art of the Con and Why People Fall for It | Psychology Today. Psychology Today; www.psychologytoday.com. https://www.psychologytoday.com/us/blog/crime-she-writes/201909/the-art-the-con-and-why-people-fall-it

Key Chapter Five Takeaways

1. The main stages of a confidence scam are Foundation Work, The Approach, The Build-Up, The Pay-Off, The Hurrah, and The In-and-In.

2. Subtler psychological confidence tricks rely on Exposure Effect, Foot-in-the-Door, and Door-in-the-Face techniques.

3. Examples of confidence scams include Get-rich-quick schemes, Gold-brick scams, Gold digging and romance scams, Humbuggery, Payoff, rag, and wire schemes, Peter Funk schemes, Ponzi schemes, and Pyramid and multi-level marketing schemes.

4. Great confidence tricksters often display the following habits: good listening, lack of boredom, agreement with political views, agreement with religious beliefs, never getting drunk, never appearing disorganized, etc.

CHAPTER SIX

HIGHLIGHTING THE DARKNESS OF GASLIGHTING

You might be familiar with the term "gaslighting," but do you know where it comes from? The term's origins can be traced back to the 1944 film Gaslight, in which a husband makes his wife believe she is insane.

One tactic he uses is to dim and brighten the gaslights and then deny that it is happening. Over the years, the term has become more widely recognized as a toxic manipulation tactic emphasizing "reality distortion."

Gaslighting is a term used to describe abusive people's mind-manipulating strategies in politics and interpersonal relationships. Specifically, it is a covert type of mental abuse designed to make people question their own memories, feelings, instincts, and sanity. The manipulator creates a false narrative they try to impose on the victim.

Psychological manipulation can become a kind of emotional abuse. Verbal abuse, domination, control, isolation, ridicule, or the exploitation of private information for humiliation are all examples of emotional abuse. This abuse occurs when the abuser attempts to gain control using manipulation and intimidation methods that severely harm the victim's self-esteem.

The victim is made to believe that they are "insane, worthless, and doomed" and that they are accountable for the abuser's words and actions. There are many types of emotional abuse.

Gaslighting is emotionally abusive manipulation that can drive a person mad. Sadly, it is also a highly efficient weapon for those with Dark Triad traits to exploit their innocent victims. Thankfully, attention is being drawn to the notion of gaslighting and gaslighters more than ever before.

The word gaslighting may be found everywhere, from clinical literature to social media. While many people may misuse the term, it is best to understand that gaslighting is a type of deceptive manipulation and that gaslighters are emotional predators. (Some people refer to them as emotional vampires!)

The main focus of this section is determining how to recognize when one is being manipulated. This also represents the book's overarching theme: awareness is the beginning of a solid defense against evil.

Once again, Gaslighting is the practice of gradually pushing a person to the point where they begin to doubt their sanity. Abusers utilize it as a psychological weapon to gain control over their victims.

Gaslighting may occur in any social, interpersonal, and professional connection. Gaslighters can range from social media celebrities to public figures to people in various positions of authority. They might be your family members, boss, co-worker, lover, spouse, or close friend. Anyone around you may gaslight you, regardless of their status in your life.

Narcissists, abusers in relationships, and cult leaders are all known to engage in gaslighting. Emotional torment can have a terrible effect on a victim. Gaslighters cannot tolerate the possibility of disagreement or criticism of their opinions. They want to control their prey and make the victims do what the they want, but, most importantly, they want their mark to agree with them.

Gaslighters utilize subtle mind games and manipulation methods to weaken their victim's sanity and stability. This is done slowly and consistently until the abuser's goal is achieved.

The victim eventually begins to distrust their own judgment and their comprehension of situations, recollections, or interpretations of events. If the gaslighting is not stopped in time, the victim begins to lose their self-worth before more dangerous damage occurs.

While other types of abuse are quickly identified, it is more challenging to notice gaslighting. This is mainly because gaslighting is often done by a person close to you, so you let your guard down with them. In addition, gaslighting may be done in various ways, gradually, until a person loses complete control.

Before uncovering the techniques behind gaslighting, it is essential to understand the reason for gaslighting. Like every other manipulation device, gaslighting also benefits the gaslighter at the victim's expense by rendering them hapless and dependent on the manipulator. It then becomes easier for the gaslighter to acquire whatever they need from their victims.

Some researchers have proposed that typical examples of gaslighting happen in three distinct stages from the victim's point of view (POV). However, not every gaslighting process involves all three.

- **Disbelief**: someone displays gaslighting behavior, but you brush it off, refusing to believe it.
- **Defense**: After a few more instances, you start to defend yourself.
- **Depression**: eventually, you accept their version of reality to avoid conflict and do whatever you can to earn their approval. But this denial of reality drains your energy, disconnecting you from yourself and leaving you feeling low and hopeless.

When I was a teenager, I found myself in many situations where I would find a party denying that an event happened as I claimed. This often surprised and infuriated me because I would clearly remember what happened.

This denial then appeared to be a puerile attempt to somehow make me appear dishonest and in the wrong. This is gaslighting in simple terms. Have you ever experienced such a thing?

Disbelief, defense, and depression may be the general themes of this deceptive evil, but how is it actually perpetrated? We shall seek these answers by exploring gaslighting in more detail.

Common gaslighting tactics

1. Lying to you

People participating in gaslighting are typically persistent and compulsive liars with narcissistic characteristics. Gaslighting is, by its very nature, dependent on lying. It is common for gaslighters to openly lie and refuse to back down or amend their statements, even when you call them out or present evidence of their lying. (*Barash, 2018*)

They say things like, "You're making stuff up," "That never occurred," or "You're insane." They are relying on their victim's desire to avoid conflict. Even when you know they are lying, they may be quite persuasive. Finally, you begin to second-guess yourself.

2. Discrediting you

Gaslighters propagate stories and talk ill about you to others. They may act concerned about you while quietly informing others that you are emotionally unstable or "crazy". Unfortunately, this strategy may be highly effective, and many support the abuser or bully without understanding the situation. (*Barash, 2018*)

Furthermore, someone who participates in gaslighting may deceive you by telling you that other people believe the same "false thing" about you. These individuals may never have said anything negative about you, but the person who is gaslighting you will try to convince you that they did.

3. Distracting you

When you ask a gaslighter a question or mention something they did or said, they will change the topic by asking you a question rather than replying to the problem at hand. This throws you off track and makes you doubt the necessity to pursue an issue when the gaslighter doesn't feel compelled to answer.

4. Minimizing your thoughts and feelings

By downplaying your emotions, the individual gaslighting you gains power over you. "Stay calm," "You're exaggerating," or "Why are you so sensitive?" are things they might say. These remarks diminish how you're feeling and thinking and suggest that you're mistaken.

When you are dealing with someone who never acknowledges your thoughts, emotions, or beliefs with any positive response, you may start to doubt the validity of the ideas yourself. Furthermore, you may never feel acknowledged or understood, which may be very lonely, embarrassing, and complicated to deal with. That is their intended goal.

5. Shifting blame

Another classic gaslighting method is blame-shifting. Every conversation you have is distorted so that you are blamed for anything that happened. Even if you try to talk about how the abuser's conduct makes you feel, they might distort the topic, so you might wonder whether you are the source of their poor behavior. They may say, for example, that if you acted differently, they wouldn't treat you like they do.

6. Denying wrongdoing

Bullies and emotional abusers are known for denying that they did anything wrong. They do this to avoid having to accept responsibility for their terrible actions. This denial can leave the target of gaslighting feeling invisible, unheard, and as if the impact on them is insignificant. This strategy also makes it difficult for the victim to recover or move on from the bullying or abuse. Notice how here, too, there is a desire to avoid responsibility. (*Barash, 2018*)

7. Using kind and loving words against you

When caught out or confronted, someone who gaslights occasionally uses gentle and kind remarks to diffuse the tension. For example, they may say something like, "You already know how much I adore you. I would never intentionally hurt you."

These are the words you want to hear. Still, they are not genuine, especially if the same atrocious and abusive conduct is repeated later. However, these kind words may be sufficient to persuade you to let them off the hook, allowing the individual to avoid accountability or repercussions for their harmful actions.

8. Rewriting history

An individual who gaslights retells stories in ways that favor them. For example, if your spouse forced you against the wall and you later discussed it, they may distort the tale and claim you stumbled and that they tried to steady you, causing you to crash into the wall.

You may start to distrust your recollection of what occurred. The goal is to confuse you or make you second-guess yourself. This tactic of historical revisionism is widespread on a societal scale too. Check how certain political groups do their very best to alter history and claim to present history through "new perspectives". Despotic regimes create artifice-driven agendas to procure power.

9. Withholding

People who gaslight may act as though they do not understand you or are unwilling to listen. They may say things like, "I don't want to hear this again" or "You're trying to confuse me." This technique is done to avoid the confrontation their victim might want, to try and resolve an issue.

By refusing to acknowledge the issue openly, victims are left with no avenues for problem resolution.

10. Countering

Even when the victim recalls events accurately, the gaslighter will question their version of events in such a way as to make the victim question their recollection. Countering is the tactic many intelligent gaslighters do very well. Remember the type of incidents I talked about earlier during my time as a teenager, where people would deny something actually happened the way I described it? This is an example of countering.

11. Blocking/diverting

Sometimes gaslighters change the subject of discussion, or they might inquire about the victim's thinking. This is usually more successful if the gaslighter's intelligence has already been acknowledged because their opinions gain automatic credibility. Unfortunately, this credibility often hurts the victim because the target often assumes that their views have less worth than the gaslighter's.

12. Trivializing

The gaslighter dismisses the victim's wants or feelings. This trivializing has many effects, including the victim beginning to internalize the trivialization. As a result, they will disregard their own ideas and thoughts and give more significance to the views of the manipulator. Once again, this cycle raises the credibility and power of the manipulator while diminishing the victim's intellect and downplaying their competence in their own eyes.

13. Forgetting/denial

The gaslighter claims to have forgotten what happened or denies making promises to the victim. (*Barash, 2018*)

Are there identifiable signs of gaslighting? While it might be challenging to pinpoint gaslighting as it occurs, specific results can be identified. Always be cautious if you ever encounter or experience the following:

● **You question your feelings and truth**: You try to persuade yourself that the treatment you receive is not that bad or that you are overly sensitive.

● **You doubt your own judgment and perceptions**: You are frightened to speak up or express your feelings. You've learned that discussing your thoughts typically makes you feel worse in the end, so you choose to remain silent.

● **You are vulnerable and insecure**: You frequently feel as if you are "walking on eggshells" with your spouse, friend, or family member. You're also tense and have low self-esteem.

● **You feel isolated and powerless**: You believe that everyone around you thinks you're "weird," "crazy," or "unstable," just as the individual who is gaslighting you claims. You feel confined and alone as a result of this.

- **You question whether you are who they claim you are**: The individual who gaslights you says things that make you feel wrong, dumb, inadequate, or mad. You may even find yourself reciting these phrases to yourself at times.

- **You're dissatisfied with yourself and who you've become**: For example, you may feel weak and submissive, even though you used to be tougher and more forceful.

- **You're perplexed**: The person gaslighting you constantly confuses you with opposing behaviors, almost as if they're Dr. Jekyll and Mr. Hyde.

- **You are concerned that you are overly sensitive**: The individual minimizes painful actions or words by claiming, "I was only kidding", or "you need tougher skin".

- **You have a feeling of impending doom**: You feel that something dreadful is going to happen when you are in the presence of this individual. This might involve feeling frightened and on alert for no apparent reason.

- **You spend a significant amount of time apologizing**: You always feel the need to apologize for who you are or what you do.

- **You have a sense of inadequacy**: You believe you are not good enough. As a result, you try to meet other people's expectations and requests, even if they are unjustified.

- **You question yourself**: You frequently doubt if you remember the specifics of prior incidents correctly. You may have even given up attempting to explain what you recall for fear of being mistaken.

- **You think others are dissatisfied with you**: You constantly apologize for what you do or who you are, expecting people to be frustrated with you or with what you have done.

- **You're wondering what's wrong with you**: At this stage, things are serious, and you constantly consider whether there's anything wrong with you. In other words, you are concerned about your mental health.

- **You have difficulty making decisions because you are afraid to do so**: You'd prefer to delegate decision-making to a spouse, friend, or close relative than make them yourself. At this level, the gaslighter has nearly achieved total victory.

What to do if you think you're being gaslit?

1. Gain some distance – physically and emotionally

When coping with gaslighting, it's natural to feel a range of powerful emotions. Anger, irritation, concern, grief, and fear are all appropriate emotions but try not to let them dictate your first reaction. Maintaining your cool might help you deal with the issue more successfully.

You may wish to refute the gaslighter's statement because, after all, it is entirely false. However, they may not give up, and your distress might encourage them to continue trying to manipulate you.

Keeping cool can also help you focus on the truth, making it difficult for their (wrong) version of events to undermine your self-confidence.

2. Save the evidence

Noting your encounters with someone who wants to gaslight you can help you immensely. You will be aware of what is happening and won't miss anything they do or say to you. In this way, if there is a confrontation, you can open your notebook or make notes on your phone and lay out the facts of what happened.

You can save texts and emails or screenshot everything written by the other party. Take photos of damaged property, if any, and summarize every conversation.

Your notes can potentially be used as proof of workplace gaslighting. When needed, take them with you; otherwise, keep them safe, without other people knowing about them.

Start to implement boundaries and do self-care exercises (like meditating, for example) while doing your investigation. This is vital because you will feel less overwhelmed and less anxious. Stress can be an enormous hindrance in dealing with the problem of gaslighting.

This is why evidence gathering is such a double-edged sword for many people.

3. Set boundaries

Make sure that there are limits that you do not let anybody cross. Doing so is necessary because you need to know where you can compromise and, more importantly, where you should never accommodate. If a violation occurs, you have to save evidence of it.

Do not depend on your recollection of events because your memory is not always reliable. On occasion, everyone remembers things differently from how something happened, and you may think, "What if it really did turn out the way they said"?

But do not doubt yourself; the manipulators want you to mistrust what you remember.

You know what happened, so repeat it calmly and confidently. Showing the gaslighters whatever evidence you have may persuade them to back off. But that is not always the case. This is why boundaries are so important. They let you know exactly what gaslighting is and should never be tolerated.

4. Get an outside perspective

Victims become involved in many situations because they do not want 'drama' or conflict. Conflicts usually happen when a problem or an issue is addressed. In case of gaslighting, seek advice and assistance from other people. When a person is being gaslighted, they lose the correct perspective of the situation.

Ask someone you trust and someone you know you can depend on to help you. Getting feedback and other perspectives from people close to you is critical. The advice you'll get can reaffirm your view of the truth and prove that you are not mad, forgetful, and are not confused.

When someone is gaslighting you at work or in different social situations, you only need to do one thing—stop interacting with that individual whenever possible. Do not engage in communication, and reduce every encounter to a minimum. If you have to communicate, ask someone else to be present during the conversation. Record the conversation whenever possible as well!

However, if you bring in other people, remember that they are not there to side with you. They are only present to watch what is happening and observe the situation from their perspective. Plus, their presence alone is a bonus because manipulators who use gaslighting find it hard to control two people simultaneously.

5. In extreme circumstances, end the relationship

If you can't solve the problem using the suggestions above, you must take drastic measures. As hard as it may seem, you will need to end the relationship and every contact you have with this person.

The "lie and denial" style of gaslighting is the first thing to take notice of. Gaslighters are liars, but they don't simply lie occasionally; lying is a way of life. Lies and denial are the weapons of choice in the arsenal that gaslighters employ to change their victims' perceptions of events. They build their abusive behavior by lying,

lying, and then lying some more. Furthermore, they don't acknowledge the falsehood when a gaslighter lies to you, and you catch them. Instead, they refute it.

Then, as the victim, you begin to doubt yourself and feel uncertain even in the most basic situations. The gaslighter aims to keep you in a perpetual state of self-doubt and bewilderment. Once you feel this way, you have no option but to seek clarification, which is just what they want. Unfortunately, seeking answers from the gaslighter often leads to a vicious cycle of abuse that makes you feel more unsure and vulnerable by the day.

We will look at an example of gaslighting to help cement our understanding of this heinous type of manipulation.

Example:

Fara overhears her boyfriend, John, trying to get another girl's phone number in the mall. Angry, she tackles him about it, but he flatly denies doing so. Even when Fara informs him that she saw him, he says she must have been hallucinating since he never sought to get any girl's number.

He does this so vehemently that Fara is confused and hesitant even when she knows she saw him, and she chooses to let it go because he denies it.

Projection is a second tactic used by gaslighters. Most gaslighters enjoy projecting; it is one of their main tools. Projecting is used to try and make the victims internalize the emotional abuse inflicted upon them. It makes the victims doubt their competence.

Gaslighters exhibit vile habits, including lying, cheating, and other deceptions, typically spreading negative thoughts, etc. Now comes the tricky part: they transfer all these habits onto you. They project their flaws onto you. Gaslighters deflect from themselves by focusing on your flaws, both real and imagined. (*Karakurt & Silver, 2013*)

You'll be too focused on defending yourself to notice that you're being accused of things the other person is doing. To make matters worse, the gaslighter will regularly project those malicious actions onto you to dominate the narrative and control your relationship. Usually, this is followed by a more egregious tactic.

In Fara and John's example, the next day, John considers Fara's claim and informs her that he feels the only reason she would accuse him of such a thing is if she cheated on him. He describes examples of times he witnessed Fara chatting to other men and how the interaction didn't appear entirely innocent, but he never blamed Fara for anything. He does it again the next day.

As he casually mentions that Fara chats to other men on the phone, it becomes part of a habit of similar accusations. Fara feels remorse and wonders why she ever believed the worst of John in the first place. In the relationship, she comes to perceive herself as a horrible person. And in the end, Fara forgets the reality of the situation and succumbs to the gaslighter's manipulative assault.

This pattern is how gaslighting typically happens. While there are many types of emotional abuse, gaslighting was used in this book because it is one of the less known types, yet its damage is horrible. General emotional abuse can lead to depression and even trauma, while gaslighting, in particular, can lead to insanity, loss of money and belongings, and maybe even worse. (*Karakurt & Silver, 2013*) Remember that the gaslighting is done because the abuser wants something from the victim that the abuser cannot get normally.

While the idea of gaslighting has been around for a while, a relatively new manipulation phenomenon will be discussed in the next chapter. This form relies on modern technology and uses the internet to manipulate victims. This new variant of manipulation could prove to be the most harmful of them all because of the massive imbalance in that realm.

References:

Abramson, K. (2014). Turning up the lights on gaslighting. Philosophical perspectives, 28, 1-30.

Barash, D. P. (2018, March 13). Gaslighting for Dummies. Psychology Today; www.psychologytoday.com. https://www.psychologytoday.com/ca/blog/pura-vida/201803/gaslighting-dummies

Catapang Podosky, P. (2021). Gaslighting, First- and Second-Order. Hypatia, 36(1), 207-227. doi:10.1017/hyp.2020.54

Cynthia A Stark, Gaslighting, Misogyny, and Psychological Oppression, The Monist, Volume 102, Issue 2, April 2019, Pages 221–235, https://doi.org/10.1093/monist/onz007

de Prado, J. G. (2021). 13 Gaslighting, Humility, and the Manipulation of Rational Autonomy. Epistemic Autonomy.

Fuchsman, K. (2019). Gaslighting. The Journal of Psychohistory, 47(1), 74-78.

Graves, C. G., & Samp, J. A. (2021). The power to gaslight. Journal of Social and Personal Relationships, 38(11), 3378–3386. https://doi.org/10.1177/02654075211026975

Johnson, V. E., Nadal, K. L., Sissoko, D. R. G., & King, R. (2021). "It's Not in Your Head": Gaslighting, 'Splaining, Victim Blaming, and Other Harmful Reactions to Microaggressions. Perspectives on Psychological Science, 16(5), 1024–1036. https://doi.org/10.1177/17456916211011963

Karakurt, G., & Silver, K. E. (2013, December 31). Emotional abuse in intimate relationships: The role of gender and age - PMC. PubMed Central (PMC); www.ncbi.nlm.nih.gov. https://www.ncbi.nlm.nih.gov/pmc/articles/PMC3876290/

Lambert, C. A. (2021, October 25). Self-Gaslighting: The Harm of Being Gaslighted. Psychology Today; www.psychologytoday.com. https://www.psychologytoday.com/ca/blog/mind-games/202110/self-gaslighting-the-harm-being-gaslighted

Mallick, M. (2021, September 16). How to Intervene When a Manager Is Gaslighting Their Employees. Harvard Business Review; hbr.org. https://hbr.org/2021/09/how-to-intervene-when-a-manager-is-gaslighting-their-employees

McBride, K. (2018, April 27). Narcissists Use "Gaslighting" to Control and Abuse. Psychology Today; www.psychologytoday.com. https://www.psychologytoday.com/ca/blog/the-legacy-distorted-love/201804/narcissists-use-gaslighting-control-and-abuse

Paola Miano, Martina Bellomare & Vincenzo Giuseppe Genova (2021) Personality correlates of gaslighting behaviours in young adults, Journal of Sexual Aggression, 27:3, 285-298, DOI: 10.1080/13552600.2020.1850893

Perkins, V., & Jason, L. A. (2022, April 11). Long COVID and Gaslighting. Psychology Today; www.psychologytoday.com. https://www.psychologytoday.com/ca/blog/the-mental-health-revolution/202204/long-covid-and-gaslighting

Pohlhaus, G. (2020). Gaslighting and Echoing, or Why Collective Epistemic Resistance is not a "Witch Hunt". Hypatia, 35(4), 674-686. doi:10.1017/hyp.2020.29

Ruíz, E. (2020). Cultural gaslighting. Hypatia, 35(4), 687-713

Sweet, P. L. (2019). The Sociology of Gaslighting. American Sociological Review, 84(5), 851–875. https://doi.org/10.1177/0003122419874843

Key Chapter Six Takeaways

1. Gaslighting is manipulation that aims to distort the target's ability to perceive reality.

2. Gaslighting usually consists of three stages: Disbelief, Defense, and Depression.

3. Standard gaslighting techniques include lying, discrediting, distracting, minimizing targets' feelings and thoughts, victim-blaming or general blame-shifting, denying wrongdoing, using kindness against the prey, rewriting history, withholding, countering, blocking/diverting, trivializing, forgetting and denial, etc.

4. Signs of gaslighting can manifest in many ways in the victim. Some of them include: questioning own judgement, perception, sanity| feeling vulnerable and insecure| feeling isolated and powerless| questions and doubts sense of self| dislikes themselves and their choices| feeling confused a lot| feeling a sense of impending danger| feeling inadequate| feels that others dislike them | wonders what's wrong with their mental health, etc.

PART III

MASS MANIPULATION

CHAPTER SEVEN

HACKING INTERNET MANIPULATION: PART 1

We have looked at the science and signs of manipulation. We then examined the most common types of interpersonal manipulation. But as vile as they are, they are not the worst kind of manipulation as far as humanity goes. By definition, interpersonal manipulation works on a small scale at the individual level.

Today, the world is advanced enough for people to be rightly terrified of the power of mass manipulation. That's right. In the contemporary world, mass manipulation is genuinely global. This topic is one of the driving forces behind the writing of this book, and thus it will be a little more detailed. Due to the extensive examination, this topic is split into two chapters.

Do you ever wonder how much your phone or laptop knows about you? Does it seem like the content that appears, like advertisements, is customized precisely to your interests? You might have heard about social media algorithms, but what are they really? There are numerous such questions surrounding the digital world. And with good reason.

The border between persuasion and manipulation on the internet is thinner than in most other places. Several university classes, particularly in social sciences and humanities, deal with the morality of the things taught to us. However, morality is a sparse commodity in the world at large. In the digital world, it is almost nonexistent in many places.

There is a fine line separating persuasion and propaganda, particularly in marketing communication lessons. One study defines online manipulation as covertly using information technology to influence another person's decision-making.

At the end of the day, each company is in the business of making money. Skillful persuasion is directly related to monetary success, and every company wants people to buy or like its products. Many companies consider the impartiality and relative obscurity associated with the internet a godsend, and this comparative anonymity is one of the main drivers of internet manipulation.

Simply put, it is far more difficult to hurt somebody if you can see them or visualize them. It goes against typical social conditioning, you see? However, on the internet, when the victim is a total stranger and worse, when algorithms do the manipulating, one does not even know who will be manipulated.

This is a horrifying thought. Internet-based manipulation allows evil to bypass the controlling inhibitions of human nature. This defining feature of the internet enables manipulators to counter whatever few inhibitions they might have. Worse, the not-really-knowing-the-target part could even incentivize them to indulge in manipulation.

Anonymity could also be why many people tend to be different in their online personas. They bank on the safety of anonymity offered by the internet. "Keyboard Warriors" is a derogatory term sometimes used to describe such people.

Internet manipulation implies using digital technology like social media algorithms for nefarious commercial, social, or political purposes. Such strategies may be used to manipulate public opinion, polarize individuals, silence political dissidents, harm business or political enemies, or improve personal or brand recognition.

Hackers, hired professionals, and regular people have all been documented to use software to manipulate the internet, typically internet bots called social bots, click bots, or vote bots. One powerful type of hacking, "cognitive-hacking," refers to a hazardous kind of cyber-attack that aims to change users' perceptions and corresponding behaviors. (*Bone, 2017*)

Yes, it is now possible to do this over the internet. This is why gaslighting was explained in the previous chapter. The digital realm has now given superpowers to the phenomenon of gaslighting and misinformation. The potential of the internet to distort and destroy the ability of the common man to perceive reality is unparalleled and indisputable.

Cognitive hacking

Cognitive hacking is defined as the practice of manipulating and falsifying information in order to change the perceptions of users. These altered perceptions cause users to alter their behavior in ways detrimental to the target. (*Cybenko et al., 2002*)

For example, a cognitive hacker might hack a notable newsperson's Twitter account and post a fraudulent tweet about a company scandal. They would then watch as users who read the tweet harm the company by selling its stock and boycotting its products.

It is difficult to defend against such information attacks because only human research, fact-checking, and astute judgment can even attempt to distinguish truth from fabricated information. As a result, research into cognitive security measures such as information verification algorithms and collaborative filtering is now crucial.

Cognitive hacking can be of three types: **disinformation, spoofing, and defacing**.

- As the word suggests, <u>disinformation is the deliberate spreading of lies to deceive and destroy</u>. The "pump-and-dump" scheme is an example of this type. In addition, artificially lowering company stock prices, then buying and selling them when the price rises is a common criminal practice. This stock market manipulation technique is not new. Still, the internet has made participating in this crime more efficient and effective.
- Spoofing is the deceptive device of duplicating an actual website intended to fool users into believing that the false website is the real one. Typically, this is done for resource theft (like confidence tricks) or disinformation purposes.
- Defacing is the deliberate maligning of websites, social media accounts, etc., for any purpose. This can range from making a statement, gaining attention, or just for personal satisfaction.

Cognitive Hacking is one form of information warfare. It is designed to control the perceptions of targeted users to make them perform detrimental actions that benefit the cognitive hacker. Information warfare is a major component of internet manipulation.

Internet and information warfare

Studies by the Center of Cuber Security in the US have defined information warfare attacks on computer systems as physical, linguistic, and semantic incursions. Disinformation provided by an enemy misleads software agents.

This spread of falsehoods is one of the most powerful weapons of warfare. In this context, cognitive hacking allows greater scope and scale to a manipulator's "reality-distorting" intentions.

Digital or information warfare can be understood as a fight between an offensive and a defensive actor over an information resource. The resource has both monetary and operational value. It could be a single computer or a vast database network of several server machines.

The resource's inherent value itself acts as a catalyst for the conflict. It is analogous to bank robbers targeting places because of their vaults. Consider now the immense value and potency of the internet, and one can understand the enormous hazards of this cyber-warfare.

Offensive information warfare usually results in greater resource availability being procured by the attacker, decreased accessibility accorded to the defense, and lower resource integrity. In this context, one should learn about a widespread internet attack protocol: denial-of-service.

A denial-of-service (DoS) attack is a type of cyber-attack where the perpetrator attempts to make a machine or network resource unavailable to its intended legitimate users. It is usually done by temporarily or indefinitely disrupting the services of a host machine connected to a network.

Denial of service is typically achieved by flooding the targeted machine or resource with unnecessary requests to overload systems and prevent some or all legitimate requests from being fulfilled.

Computer and network security, or their vulnerability, poses significant problems to our rapidly changing information society and economy. The diversity and complexity of cybersecurity threats parallel the variety and complexity of information technology. As technology becomes more advanced, so do the technological threats.

This should come as no surprise because it is analogous to developments in warfare occurring since the beginning of humanity. Stronger shields often caused the development of more robust and sharper blades. When full plate armor replaced chain-mail hauberks, arming swords became longswords which were then replaced by war hammers and pole-axes.

Eventually, plate armor itself became obsolete when gunpowder weapons became the norm. Kevlar soon provided some defensive protection, but then armor-piercing rounds were born. The contest between offense and defense is nothing new, and their development is closely interlinked. Things are no different in the digital world. There are many different types of cyber-attacks.

An attacker, for example, can download and utilize files containing sensitive information such as credit card numbers. The physical presence of users of the attacked system is not even required for such an assault to succeed. On the other hand, a cognitive attack necessitates a change in user behavior, which is done by influencing their perspective of reality.

A digital psychological assault cannot succeed unless human users modify their behavior. The changing activities of users are an essential goal-post in the sequence of a cognitive assault.

Therefore, for manipulators, it becomes vital that they use mechanisms to learn about user activities and behaviors. This is because, without this knowledge, they cannot hope to modify the thoughts of their targets. Does this requirement sound familiar? Remember the first step in the confidence trick?

It has been seen how Denial-of-Service attacks aim to control and steal digital resources that belong to others. Cognitive Hacking has also been explored, where manipulators attempt to assault the ability of victims to perceive reality through the digital world/internet. Simply put, internet manipulation allows for confidence scams and gaslighting manipulation on a massive scale without even needing to know the victim personally. The power imbalance created here is so dangerous that individual sovereignty is now more viciously threatened than ever before.

Unfortunately, the worst part of internet manipulation is not the expanded reach the Web provides to individual manipulators. The internet is also a hyper-effective vehicle for government propaganda.

State-sponsored internet propaganda

Ongoing worldwide media investigations have revealed operational information regarding espionage agencies' global surveillance of both foreign and domestic persons. The most famous claims are primarily based on a collection of top-secret papers revealed by ex-NSA contractor Edward Snowden. Snowden worked for Booz Allen Hamilton, one of the major defense and intelligence companies in the United States.

In addition to a treasure of federal records from the United States, Snowden's stockpile is said to contain thousands of intelligence files from Australia, the United Kingdom, Canada, and New Zealand, which he obtained through the exclusive "Five Eyes" network. ["Five Eyes" refers to the intelligence agencies' shared collaboration of five Anglophonic/English speaking countries- USA, UK, Canada, Australia, and New Zealand]

The first of Snowden's documents, published simultaneously by The Washington Post and The Guardian in June 2013, deservedly drew widespread public attention.

These media stories have highlighted the ramifications of various secret treaties signed by many western countries' intelligence organizations in their quest to conduct global monitoring. One example is the UKUSA/Five Eyes signal intelligence sharing secret agreement. (*White, 2010*)

This agreement goes back to the middle of World War 2. Yet, even the Australian Prime Minister did not know this until the 1970s. The general public did not know about it until the 21st century. The full text of the agreement was publicly released by the United Kingdom and the United States on June 25, 2010, for the first time in history. (*Newly Released GCHQ Files: UKUSA Agreement, 2010*)

In order to destroy targets' reputations, many tactics were used. These include introducing false material onto the internet and manipulating online discourse and activism. Typical methods used to do these include posting material to the Internet and falsely attributing it to someone else. Other methods involve pretending to be a victim of the target individual whose reputation is to be destroyed and posting "negative information" on various forums.

There have been numerous revelations about such espionage. Der Spiegel, for example, disclosed how the German Federal Intelligence Service (BND) transfers "vast quantities of intercepted data to the NSA." At the same time, Swedish Television revealed how the National Defence Radio Establishment (FRA) supplied the NSA with data from its cable collection under a secret peace treaty from 1954 for bilateral cooperation on monitoring.

Other countries with security and intelligence agencies involved in global surveillance include Australia (ASD), the United Kingdom (GCHQ), Canada (CSE), Denmark (PET), France (DGSE), Germany (BND), Italy (AISE), the Netherlands (AIVD), Norway (NIS), Spain (CNI), Switzerland (NDB), Singapore (SID), and Israel (ISNU), which receives raw, unfiltered data from the NSA.

On June 14, 2013, prosecutors in the United States accused Edward Snowden of treason and theft of state property. The Russian government granted him temporary asylum for one year in late July 2013, worsening Russia-United States ties.

Towards the end of October 2013, British Prime Minister David Cameron sent a DA-Notice to The Guardian, warning it not to publish any future leaks. The Metropolitan Police Service in the United Kingdom conducted a criminal investigation into the disclosure in November 2013. Alan Rusbridger, the editor of The Guardian, stated in December 2013, "We have published, I think, 26 papers so far out of the 58,000 we've seen".

You may wonder why we are discussing all these details about the Edward Snowden issue here. This is not about politics. However, no proper discussion of mass manipulation is honest, accurate, or complete without exploring the traditional and most common source of mass manipulation: the government/state.

Manipulation is dark power, and what entity epitomizes power more than the government? The purpose of this book is education, and it is, therefore, essential to discuss the Snowden disclosures because of their world-altering impact.

The level to which the media stories have correctly educated the public is debatable. The nefarious power of its detractors has prevented the total dissemination of this incredibly valuable information. In January 2014, then US President Obama stated that "the spectacular manner in which these leaks have come out has frequently shed more heat than light", while others have pointed out that many of the Snowden papers do not pertain to domestic spying.

And yet, they all seem to want to destroy Snowden for stealing things that supposedly "spread more heat than light" and do not "pertain to domestic spying.".Why is "darkness" so concerned about something that spreads only a little light?

The establishment claims that the strategic harm caused by the revelations weighs more heavily on the US and British defense establishments than the civic public gain. (Surprised?)

In its first review of these revelations, the Pentagon decided that Snowden performed the largest "theft" of US secrets in US history. Former GCHQ director Sir David Omand called Snowden's leak the "most devastating loss to British intelligence ever."

The question then ought to be whether the loss of intelligence for the state is a gain in intelligence for the public. Logically, the answer ought to be obvious. If knowledge is the most critical thing in a conflict, access to knowledge is the most crucial tool the public can have.

Individual freedom rests on the ability of every sovereign individual to make their own decisions. But no conclusion can ever be considered wise if it is made without having all the required information. Access to knowledge is vital to resist tyranny in the modern era where power imbalances grossly favor the collective.

To better understand the severity of this danger, let us look at censorship. The government traditionally enforced censorship, sometimes even with physical force. However, the nature of censorship has changed with the arrival of the internet and new information technologies.

Internet censorship

Internet censorship is the restriction or suppression of what may be accessed, published, or seen on the internet, enforced by government authorities or at the initiative of internet service providers (ISPs). Internet censorship thus limits what information may and may not be posted or seen on the internet.

Organizations and individuals could enroll in self-censorship for moral, religious, or commercial reasons. Censorship could also be used to make people adhere to social norms, bow to mobocratic intimidation, or conform to things out of fear of legal or other repercussions.

The number of internet restrictions varies by nation. While some countries have limited internet censorship, others go so far as to block access to information such as news and even repress and quiet public debate. This is analogous to the banning of cinema, barring of free press, and other similar practices in the strict communist nations of the 20th Century.

Even today, the World Press Freedom Index shows that countries like Vietnam, North Korea, China, Turkmenistan, Laos, and Cuba rank at the bottom of the freedom list with countries like Saudi Arabia, Yemen, Bahrain, Libya, Syria, Iran, Iraq, etc. This is quite insightful. Communist countries seem to rank alongside theocratic autocracies when it comes to a lack of press freedom. Two polar opposite political ideologies are equal when it comes to press censorship.

The idea of state manipulation of the internet and information, in general, mustn't be condoned. But it should not be assumed that on its own, a free press is a guarantor of free and unblemished information flow. This will be discussed in subsequent chapters.

Internet filtering can also occur in response to or in preparation for events such as elections, demonstrations, and riots. Censorship has intensified as a result of the events of Arab Spring. Other forms of censorship feature the use of copyright, defamation, harassment, and obscene material allegations to restrict information.

Support for and resistance to internet control differ as well. According to a 2012 Internet Society study, seventy-one percent of respondents believed that "censorship must exist in some form on the Internet." This is both problematic and despicable.

Yet, in the same study, eighty-six percent said that "free expression on the Internet should be safeguarded." These opinions are contradictory but can be explained logically. The vast majority of people believe in free speech as long as what is being spoken about is not detrimental to society as they saw fit.

The controversy surrounding internet censorship is primarily based on the fundamental human right of free speech. This has influenced the concept of universal human rights and the understanding of liberty and individual sovereignty. According to Global Web Index, approximately 400 million users use virtual private networks to avoid censorship or improve user privacy. This is a fascinating piece of information.

"Hate Speech" manipulation

Prohibiting Hate Speech is a form of severe censorship and an infringement of the fundamental human right to free expression. The belief that public conversation should function as a marketplace of ideas is one argument for the virtues of free speech. Many people find it illogical and hypocritical to censor hate speech. (*Strossen, 2018*)

This viewpoint, commonly attributed to mid-nineteenth-century philosopher John Stewart Mill, contends that hate speech is an inescapable component of the larger current of free speech. This view holds that everything must be disputable to decide what is true and wrong.

This idea even prioritizes the advancement of the community over individual preferences. In On Liberty, Mill writes, "They [an individual] have no right to resolve the matter for all humanity and to exclude all other people from the means of judgment... All stifling of debate is based on the idea of infallibility."

In this passage, Mill argues that hate speech is necessary as a stepping stone to the truth. Denying people the right to analyze remarks because they feel such words are hurtful is a unilateral and incorrect decision that will eventually be detrimental to the communal benefit. Furthermore, it brings unwarranted subjectivity and emotions to the precious realm of objectivity and logic.

Although some people believe that speech may and should be controlled in specific circumstances, others are adamant that all communication, even hate speech, is necessary for the community's growth and development. Several human rights activists, free speech advocates, and academics have spoken out against the practice of banning hate speech. (*Conklin, 2020*)

According to several prominent civil rights campaigners, measures to ban hate speech pretend to have the purpose of safeguarding the most vulnerable. However, they are ineffectual and may have the opposite result: underprivileged and ethnic minorities being prosecuted for breaching hate speech legislation. (*Strossen, 2018*) By mollycoddling the vulnerable in a way that prolongs their vulnerability, the misguided supporters of censorship are harming everybody around.

Hate speech works primarily on the idea that hate is to be banned. That is the most malignant of assertions. Does the concept of individual sovereignty give someone the freedom to love? Then, what about the freedom to hate what one rightly finds malevolent?

Laws against hate speech constitute viewpoint discrimination (which is forbidden by First Amendment case law in the United States) because the legal system punishes some viewpoints but not others. So, is hate speech the actual crime, or is it the criminal censoring of speech?

Additionally, limiting hate speech is often based on dubious philosophical and pseudo-scientific ideas, and the practice is reminiscent of authoritarian governments' efforts to control their populations' beliefs. This false justification for curbing free speech is reprehensible and extremely dangerous. (*Chomsky, 1989*)

As the digital age progresses, the application of free speech becomes even more contentious and vulnerable as new modes of communication and restrictions emerge. One example is the Golden Shield Project, an initiative of the Chinese government's Ministry of Public Security that filters potentially unfavorable data from foreign countries.

In fact, there are certain benefits to "hate speech" that are often neglected. It has been said that permitting hate speech offers a more accurate picture of the human condition and opportunities to influence people's beliefs. It highlights specific persons who should be avoided in certain situations. (*Conklin, 2022*)

This needs to be reiterated. Uncensored speech is the surest way to observe, preserve, and utilize truth and reality. In other words, banning hate speech is a form of "reality distortion" and manipulation because it propagates falsehood, lies, and deception. Think about how this mirrors gaslighting.

We looked at how speech is being targeted on the internet. But what happens to the people who are targeted? How are their lives manipulated? Who plays a significant role when it comes to manipulation?

Big Tech, cancel culture, and deplatforming

Big Tech companies often provide services to users worldwide, allowing companies to influence user behavior and obtain control over user data. Concerns over monopolistic behavior prompted antitrust investigations by the U.S. Department of Justice & Federal Trade Commission and the European Commission.

Commentators have raised concerns about these businesses' influence on privacy, market dominance, free expression and censorship, national security, and law enforcement. It has been hypothesized that living in the digital world outside of the environment built by the firms may be impossible.

Deplatforming, recognized as no-platforming, is defined as an attempt to ban a group or individual by removing the platforms (including speaking establishments or webpages) used to share ideas or information. It can also be understood as the activity/practice of preventing someone holding viewpoints viewed as inappropriate or offensive from contributing to a forum or debate, particularly by obstructing them on a specific website.

Deplatforming of invited speakers

The prohibition of speakers on college campuses in the United States stretches back to the 1940s. This was accomplished by measures enacted by the universities themselves. For example, the University of California introduced a policy like this one, named the Speaker Ban, which was established in university statutes under the leadership of President Robert Gordon Sproul and targeted communists primarily, but not solely.

According to one rule, "the University claimed the authority to exclude untrained people or those who would use it as a platform for propaganda from the exploitation of its prestige." This restriction was invoked in 1951 to prevent socialist Max Shachtman from presenting at the University of California, Berkeley. Former US Vice President Henry A. Wallace was barred from speaking at UCLA in 1947 due to his views on US Cold War policies. Malcolm X was banned from appearing at Berkeley as a religious leader in 1961.

Deplatforming efforts to disbar or otherwise stop controversial speakers from speaking on college campuses have been made against controversial speakers who have been asked to speak. The British National Union of Students instituted its No Platform policy in 1973. South African ambassador Glenn Babb's tours to Canadian university campuses in the mid-1980s were met with protest by anti-apartheid students.

Recent occurrences in the United States also include demonstrators' March 2017 disruption of political science professor Charles Murray's public address at Middlebury College. After criticism from an LGBT student group, University of Central Oklahoma students revoked a speaking request to creationist Ken Ham in February 2018.

A handful of unruly "demonstrators" at Lewis & Clark Law School attempted to disrupt a speech by visiting professor Christina Hoff Sommers in March 2018. Adam Carolla and Dennis Prager recorded their own exclusion and that of others in the invaluable 2019 movie No Safe Spaces.

The foundation for Individual Rights in Education, from February 2020, observed 469 dis-invitation or disruption efforts at American Campuses. This speech advocacy group explored both unsuccessful dis-invitation attempts and successful dis-invitations. Surprisingly, the trend seems to have reversed since the Cold War era in terms of who is targeted by the deplatforming now.

Nowadays, the deplatforming and attempted disruption of speakers seem to be done by radical leftists. This can be inferred by looking at the most common targets of such disruption.

Deplatforming in social media

Deplatforming has been amplified with the prevalence of social media today. For example, Reddit suspended multiple groups for breaking the site's anti-harassment policies at the beginning of 2015.

A study published in the journal Proceedings of the ACM on Human-Computer Interaction in 2017 found that the ban delivered a variety of 'valuable purposes' for the company (Reddit) and that the users that were a part of the forbidden subreddits left the site. Those that stayed dramatically reduced the use of 'hate speech.'" Surprisingly, communities that acquired these deplatformed users did not see a rise in hate speech.

Logically, the most likely answer for this would be the echo chamber effect. Hate speech is often conflict speech, which occurs where there is dissension, disagreement, and conflict. But if people move into areas where there are only like-minded people, the potential for conflict is diminished. Ergo, the potential for conflict in speech will also decrease.

Reddit also banned two large online pro-Trump groups in June 2020 and January 2021 for violating the website's safety and harassment regulations.

On May 2, 2019, Facebook and its subsidiary Instagram announced the removal of "risky or dangerous individuals and groups," like Milo Yiannopoulos, Nation of Islam Leader Louis Farrakhan, Laura Loomer, Paul Joseph Watson, Alex Jones, and the organization under him, InfoWars, etc.

Following the assault of the US Capitol in 2021, Twitter suspended Donald Trump and an additional 70,000 accounts allegedly associated with the incident and the far-right organization QAnon.

Harassment and threats to employment

Attempts to silence problematic speakers through different types of personal harassment, such as doxing, the filing of bogus emergency reports, and objections or petitions to third parties, have also been used as deplatforming strategies. Protesters have sought to get speakers banned from projects or sacked from their professions in some circumstances.

Students at the University of the Arts in Philadelphia, for instance, filed an online petition in 2019 demanding that a teacher, Camille Paglia, be removed from the Arts faculty and replaced by a queer person of color. According to Conor Friedersdorf of The Atlantic, "it is uncommon for student activists to urge that a tenured academic member at their own university should be refused a platform". And they publicly endeavored to indulge in illegal discrimination by calling for recruitment policies that are prejudiced and biased: the very essence of discrimination.

The irony is that Paglia herself is a tenured professor who identifies as transgender and has long been vocal on the "matters of sex, gender identification, and sexual assault". This is a truly bizarre incident of cancel culture.

Cancel Culture

Cancel culture is a modern term for ostracism in which someone is pushed out of professional and social circles: online, on social networks, or in person. Those subjected to this social exclusion are said to have been "canceled." The term "cancel culture" has malicious connotations and is frequently used in free speech and censorship discussions.

Cancel culture is a variation of the term "call-out culture." It is commonly described as boycotting or shunning someone perceived to have done or talked inappropriately. It is analogous to the practice of Untouchability, famously practiced in India for centuries before the modern era, because it targets the social destruction of an individual.

Many say that cancel culture hinders pure and intellectual public conversation. Some misguided people think that cancellation requests are a type of free expression in and of themselves and that they encourage accountability. The truth is that this exercise of mobocratic malevolence is often targeted at innocent citizens exercising their legal and moral right to freedom of speech.

This mass manipulation stratagem uses mob hostility to boost the predators' power and control with the help of the internet. In modern democracies, voters call the shots or are supposed to. Voter suppression through cancel culture and behavioral modification through intimidation are all manipulation tactics tried and tested over the last century with the explicit intention of corrupting democracies.

To better understand how the internet is only a tool in such games of power, it is vital to learn about a Nobel laureate named Ivan Petrovich Pavlov. Pavlov was a Russian physiologist who was awarded the Nobel Prize for Medicine. He is known for his psychological work in classical conditioning.

Pavlov's theories became the mainstay of conditioning studies which involved behavior modification. One of the assertions of this process includes manipulating behavior with a sufficiently strong stimulus. Fear is one of the most potent stimuli. Cancel culture using the internet is a clear case of using fear to manipulate and condition the victims into surrender and make them submit to the whims of the manipulator. (*Dimsdale, 2021*)

This chapter was designed to explain the direct forms of internet manipulation that various entities indulged in. This is more overt and uses force to hurt the intended targets.

Along with overt manipulation, the internet can also be used for a more covert form of manipulation. This hidden deception is so potent because it can be done using visual design and automation. So get ready to meet Dark Patterns.

References:

Anderson, J., Vogel, E. A., & Rainie, L. (2021, February 18). Experts Say the 'New Normal' in 2025 Will Be Far More Tech-Driven, Presenting More Big Challenges. Pew Research Center: Internet, Science & Tech; www.pewresearch.org. https://www.pewresearch.org/internet/2021/02/18/experts-say-the-new-normal-in-2025-will-be-far-more-tech-driven-presenting-more-big-challenges/

Bone, J. (2017). Cognitive Hack: The New Battleground in Cybersecurity, the Human Mind. Auerbach Publications.

Burr, C., Cristianini, N., & Ladyman, J. (2018). An Analysis of the Interaction Between Intelligent Software Agents and Human Users. Minds and machines, 28(4), 735–774. https://doi.org/10.1007/s11023-018-9479-0

Chomsky, N. (1989). Necessary Illusions: Thought Control in Democratic Societies. South End Press.

Colin M. Gray and Shruthi Sai Chivukula. 2021. "That's dastardly ingenious": Ethical Argumentation Strategies on Reddit. Proc. ACM Hum.-Comput. Interact. 5, CSCW1, Article 70 (April 2021), 25 pages.

Conklin, M. (2020, June 1). Hate Speech: An Analysis of Free Speech Advocacy by Michael Conklin :: SSRN. Hate Speech: An Analysis of Free Speech Advocacy by Michael Conklin :: SSRN; papers.ssrn.com. https://papers.ssrn.com/sol3/papers.cfm?abstract_id=3591433

Conklin, M. (2022, April 29). Anti-Semitism and the Overlooked Benefits of Allowing "Hate Speech" by Michael Conklin :: SSRN. Anti-Semitism and the Overlooked Benefits of Allowing "Hate Speech" by Michael Conklin :: SSRN; papers.ssrn.com. https://papers.ssrn.com/sol3/papers.cfm?abstract_id=4094129

Cybenko, G., Giani, A., & Thompson, P. (2002, August 1). Cognitive Hacking: A Battle for the Mind. CSDL | IEEE Computer Society; www.computer.org. https://www.computer.org/csdl/magazine/co/2002/08/r8050/13rRUxYrbPz

Dimsdale, J. E. (2021). Dark Persuasion: A History of Brainwashing From Pavlov to Social Media. Yale University Press.

Eviette M., Simpson A. (2021) Towards Models for Privacy Preservation in the Face of Metadata Exploitation. In: Friedewald M., Schiffner S., Krenn S. (eds) Privacy and Identity Management. Privacy and Identity 2020. IFIP Advances in Information and Communication Technology, vol 619. Springer, Cham.

Fussell, S. (2019, August 5). The Endless, invisible persuasion tactics of the internet. The Atlantic. Retrieved April 14, 2022, from https://www.theatlantic.com/technology/archive/2019/08/how-dark-patterns-online-manipulate-shoppers/595360/

Kaminska, I. (2020, August 17). Cognitive hacking as the new disinformation frontier. Financial Times; www.ft.com. https://www.ft.com/content/52535b2b-cb23-4ab6-ac66-2859cf9d1ae9

Newly released GCHQ files: UKUSA Agreement. (2010, June 0). Newly Released GCHQ Files: UKUSA Agreement; www.nationalarchives.gov.uk. https://www.nationalarchives.gov.uk/ukusa/

Norton-Taylor, R. (2010, June 24). Not so secret: deal at the heart of UK-US intelligence. The Guardian; www.theguardian.com. https://www.theguardian.com/world/2010/jun/25/intelligence-deal-uk-us-released

Strossen, N. (2018). Hate: Why We Should Resist It with Free Speech, Not Censorship. Oxford University Press.

White, A. (2010, June 29). How a Secret Spy Pact Helped Win the Cold War. TIME.Com; content.time.com. http://content.time.com/time/nation/article/0,8599,2000262,00.html

Key Chapter Seven Takeaways

1. Internet manipulation is digital manipulation. It is mass manipulation where the lack of a direct personal interaction can remove all inhibitions and encourages more people to participate in manipulation over the internet.

2. The goals of the manipulators usually remain the same in Internet manipulation as in other manipulation. They try to steal their victims' resources and may engage in reality-distorting tactics.

3. Information warfare is a major component of internet manipulation. While internet access has increased access to knowledge, it has also provided more ways to create disinformation.

4. Two main types of internet manipulation include overt Denial-of-Service attacks aimed at stealing resources and covert Cognitive-Hacking attacks aimed at altering victims' behaviour.

5. One of the most dangerous aspects of internet manipulation is state-driven propaganda. The general public is left ignorant of reality and the truth about the world. It has even led to the erosion of national boundaries, further empowering national governments at the expense of the individual citizen.

6. Internet manipulation has led to massive destruction of privacy −the true evidence of individual freedom.

7. The internet has also been used to indulge in censorship where individual voices are censored. This has given both governments and corporations massive power to manipulate the public to enforce their specific agenda.

8. "Hate Speech" manipulation over the internet is an excellent example of thought-policing, enforcing groupthink, and using mobocratic elements to manipulate the public into conforming against their free expression: attacking free speech.

9. The internet also allows the Big Tech firms to enjoy their monopoly and the resulting massive power imbalance between them and the average consumer. They, too, can indulge in censorship, cancel culture, etc.

10. The internet has been used to manipulate others through fear using methods such as deplatforming, etc. Cancel Culture has led to the ruin of innocent lives, the destruction of reputation, job loss, and the violation of individuals' freedom.

CHAPTER EIGHT

HACKING INTERNET MANIPULATION – PART 2: DARK PATTERNS AND MANIPULATIVE DESIGN.

George Orwell's masterpiece, 1984, has been studied for many decades now, and it serves as a cautionary tale about how fragile the existence of individual freedoms is. Human rights are considered universal and taken for granted when they are neither universal nor always granted. By now, it must be evident that targeting individual rights is a mainstay of psychological manipulation.

This leads us to a new manipulative concept: Dark Patterns. Social media amplify the power of crowd intimidation and falsehoods. This can happen because social media and the internet have features that enable the creation of unique manipulation tactics that you should be aware of and wary of. On that note, let's explore the visual design-based manipulative methods called Dark Patterns.

Dark Patterns.

A Dark Pattern is defined as a carefully crafted user interface that has been purposely made to mislead consumers into doing things (such as buying expensive insurance with their actual purchase or signing up for unwarranted recurring fees). The way a website is designed visually can actually influence the site's viewers. Welcome to the confidence scams of the digital world.

On July 28, 2010, user-experience (UX) designer Harry Brignull registered darkpatterns.org, which has been called a pattern library with the explicit objective of recognizing and condemning nefarious user interfaces.

In a broader sense, dark patterns replace user experience and value in favor of shareholder value through vile methods. (*Brignull, 2012*)

Dark Patterns and its study is one of the specialties of this book. In fact, it was during my research on Dark Patterns that I initially decided to do a book on Dark Psychology. Dark Patterns use several techniques.

1. Privacy Zuckering: −This is a technique whereby users are tricked into providing more information than they originally wanted. Users may provide this information unknowingly or as a result of tactics that conceal or postpone the choice to opt out of sharing personal data. This is also compounded by the Auto-Fill option provided by many internet browsers.

While Auto-Fill is designed to save you time and effort, it also makes it easier for websites to gain your private information. For example, all you may see at the top is the column for your name; when you click on that, the Auto-Fill will fill up all the following information based on the data you have had saved.

Imagine then how easy it would be to collect information you had no intention of imparting. How many of us go through every part of a webpage before we do what we want and depart?

The ease with which our privacy gets eroded in such ways could be why many organizations have begun to try and legislate against such practices. For instance, the California Consumer Privacy Act has authorized laws that prohibit this.

2. Trick questions: −While filling out a form, you answer a question that fools you into providing an incorrect response. At first glance, the question appears to ask one thing. But it is really asking something else, which becomes more evident when you read carefully. Such trick questions are nothing new in the real world, but now they have the scope to manipulate large groups of people using the power of the internet.

3. Sneak into basket:−You try to buy something, but somewhere along the way, the site slips an extra item into your basket, frequently using an opt-out right-click or checkbox on a previous page, which can be easily missed. This is analogous to how in real life, salespeople withhold information from customers and lead them to buy things without their knowledge.

4. Price comparison prevention: −The vendor makes it difficult for you to examine the prices of different items, preventing you from making an informed selection. This can be done by deliberately presenting muddled information or, more effectively, by making it harder to get comparative prices by disabling the ability to highlight-copy-paste text on the webpage.

This disabling is done because one of the easiest ways to research information online is by highlighting something and right-clicking it. On the popped-up mini-window, we click on search-Google-for-[highlighted text].

But suppose that feature is disabled on the website by not allowing for highlighting. In that case, it makes research harder, and the extra effort needed might discourage many customers. They may go ahead with the transaction without further checking to avoid extra effort and time spent.

5. Hidden costs: −You reach the last stage of the checkout process only to realize that some unexpected expenses have surfaced, such as shipping charges, tax, and so on. Consider it fortunate if you realize it because you can then take appropriate action. But in many cases, people fail to recognize this and will spend the extra money.

One method this is done is by deliberately using false and extra money in the name of tax. How many of us frankly calculate the tax amount presented to us to see if it is accurate? Do we even know how it is calculated?

Here is one real-life example. While using a famous food delivery website, I had a 30% discount offer. After the total purchase amount came to about 50 dollars, the tax was calculated at 8 dollars (16%), so the total became 58$. When I put in the discount code, I expected the first purchase total to become 35 dollars after the 30% discount of 15 dollars. After the new tax of 5.6 dollars was added, the new total should have been 40.6 dollars.

But then I saw that the final total was still 43 dollars. In other words, they had added the whole 50 dollars' tax amount to the discounted sum of 35 dollars. This is nothing but cheating. The tax had to be based on 35 dollars, but they were showing the greater tax amount. Since I was aware, I caught on to it. Needless to say, I spread this information to as many people as possible, and I have never used the site again.

Yet consider how many innocent people fall for such malicious and criminal deception daily?

6. Disguised ads:−Advertisements that masquerade as other types of information or navigation to entice you to act on them. False and misleading ads will be discussed later in more detail as they are a vast subject in the field of manipulation.

7. Forced continuity: −This happens when your free trial period with a service expires, and your credit card is secretly debited without notice. This may be exacerbated by making it tough to terminate the membership.

How many of us keep track of the end date of all our subscriptions to cancel them before they are renewed? It has been found that over 92% of people do not actively know all the subscriptions they are paying for.

8. Friend Spam:–The website or app may request your email address or social network permissions under the guise that it would be used for a beneficial consequence (meeting friends). Later the website spams all of your contacts with a message claiming to be from you. This is very common. Have you noticed that when you use your social media account or your email to log in to a website, you sometimes see a pop-up where it says something like "this website/app" wants to access your "contacts/friends list/something else" and you have to click either Accept or Deny? Most folks click Accept without a second thought. This is what this Dark Pattern technique is all about. This method of using your email to login to third-party websites without needing a separate account at the website itself, is relatively new. On the surface, it is supposed to help consumers by reducing the number of digital profiles they need to create. But the reality is that this benefits companies far more than it does the individual.

9. Bait-and-switch: –These schemes promote a free (or drastically reduced-priced) product or service that is unavailable or only offered in limited numbers. Then, following the announcement of the product's unavailability, the page displays comparable alternatives at a higher cost or of lesser quality. This uses the scarcity principle and combines that with the manipulation of people's gullibility.

10. Confirm-shaming: This method uses shame to motivate people. For instance, websites may phrase the choice to refuse an email newsletter so that users are shamed into accepting it. Most examples have messages like "If you do not want to better yourself, go ahead and unsubscribe" or something along those lines.

11. Misdirection: –This is prevalent among software installers, providing the user with a button that seems like a conventional continue button. A dark design would include an "I accept the terms" button that would prompt the user to accept the conditions of an application unrelated to the one they are attempting to install.

Because the user will often accept the conditions out of habit, the irrelevant software can then be installed. The installer creators usually do this because the writers of the unrelated software pay for each download installed. The alternate path in the download, which allows the user to bypass installing the unrelated product, is considerably less clearly highlighted and may even appear counter-intuitive.

12. Roach Motel: –A roach motel or trammel-net design, allows for a simple passage in but an arduous journey out. Businesses that demand subscribers to mail their opt-out or termination requests are examples of the Roach Motel concept in action.

Online businesses often use manipulative designs (dark patterns) to persuade customers to buy goods and subscriptions, spend a longer time on-site, or passively allow the collection of their personal data. Customers have to be conscious of the deceptiveness of dark patterns to be safe from the allure of such designs. But even if they are aware, will they be able to withstand the manipulation?

According to a poll of 406 people conducted in Luxembourg, many people are typically aware of the effect that deceptive designs may have on their online behavior. Being conscious, however, does not provide consumers with the capacity to counter such effects. (*Lenzini et al., 2021*) This information indicates that those who were aware did not care that the designs were deceiving them, and those who did care were unequipped to deal with it. So, Dark Patterns worked despite people knowing about it.

Similarly, it was also discovered that respondents, particularly younger ones, frequently recognize the "darkness" of some designs but are dubious of the actual harm they may cause. That seems the cruelest aspect of it. Imagine knowing about manipulation but not finding it to be of any import because of the ignorance about potential outcomes.

This has to change. The pervasiveness of deceptive techniques in internet businesses is gaining attention. This can be attributed to the immense power of dark psychological practices using the internet. Manipulative tactics may now be executed at little cost and on a massive scale, with unparalleled sophistication and efficacy in interactive, invasive, and adaptable settings, thanks to advances in information technology. (*Cara, 2020*)

Such online practices attempt to influence purchase decisions and nudge people to spend significant amounts of time on a service (thus intensifying data collection to fuel the so-called attention economy). These practices also attempt to trick users into accepting privacy-invasive features, thereby undermining their right to personal information protection and exposing them to privacy harm. (*Toth & Clifford, 2021*)

Online manipulation undermines legal safeguards and deprives unsuspecting persons of their ability to make autonomous decisions. Moreover, the difficulty of unsubscribing from a service has a specific monetary impact: it causes people to spend money they did not mean to pay.

However, dark patterns can create other types of damage as well. This harm could come in the form of emotional manipulation. Examples of such practices include a website displaying a countdown clock on an offer to speed up a customer's decision-making. In that case, the passing time does not influence the sale or usage of the product or service except as a means to generate an emotional reaction in the consumer. This "limited-time" device is intended to provoke a panic-type emotional response in the customer in the hopes that they will function emotionally instead of rationally.

A loss of privacy could also be the intended outcome. For instance, some websites and apps ask users to disable data collection in two distinct settings rather than making privacy settings quickly accessible. Thus, dark patterns can affect one's money, liberty, and even time. (*Fritsch, 2017*)

Because there is usually a power imbalance between users and companies, it is difficult for people to protect themselves from misleading design tactics constantly. Dark patterns allow users to be deceived into doing things they don't want to do, robbing them of their fundamental freedom to choose freely. (*Luguri & Strahilevitz, 2021*)

And here is another reason why Dark Patterns are so effective. Typical internet malice comes from general malware like viruses, adware, spyware, etc., against which people use antiviruses and other software. However, here the malcontents do not have to enter your computer to do damage. Instead, you are entering their domain, and they are tricking you through design features.

These murky but widespread methods are unanimously condemned. However, they are still widely practiced today, even by some of the world's most well-known and largest corporations, with no severe consequences.

Although some businesses are found out, such as LinkedIn, which was fined thirteen million dollars for tricking its customers into spamming their connections, most brands and organizations get away with it. Even LinkedIn still functions as usual, and one hopes that they do not continue to trick their patrons.

Unfortunately, in the absence of tougher laws, firms will continue to use deceptive techniques for short-term and long-term profits. These practices allow them to forego using any legitimate business or product strategies to build their user base and income. This is so because doing it legitimately is usually much harder and takes longer to succeed. (*Fitton et.al, 2021*)

Why does a book on manipulation and dark psychology have to consider Cancel Culture, Propaganda, Censorship, etc., and Dark Patterns when studying internet manipulation? Well, one of the targets of mass manipulation is the beliefs and behaviors of the population at large. The key is that mass manipulation is intended to steal more than one's finances; people's autonomy is on the line too.

This problem is getting worse as the relevant technologies become more advanced. Of particular note is a field that has been gaining tremendous attention. As usual, many scientists and activists clamoring for its continued progress often ridicule and try to cancel people who mention the idea that "AI could develop a conscience."

There is just one problem, though. In all the hue and cry about conscience and ethics, nobody sane denies the remarkable capacity of AI and Neural Networks in information processing and, consequently, their undeniable impact on mass psychological manipulation.

And how real is this much-glorified and vastly lauded individual freedom? How long will it survive when 1984-esque Big Brother comes alive through artificial-intelligence-enabled technologies? This is done by combining dark patterns with machine learning. (SKYNET, anyone?). AI does not have to be conscious for it to be used by vile people to conduct mass malevolence.

This chapter explains the algorithmic tools of internet manipulation and how they are implemented. Privacy and surveillance experts are increasingly concerned that data collectors will exploit the information they acquire about our actions, preferences, hobbies, and incomes to control us.

Consider this: Lately, investigative journalists revealed that Facebook allows marketers to target vulnerable teens when they feel "worthless" and "insecure." In addition, companies in the "sharing economy," such as the ride-hailing giant Uber, have investigated ways to influence both their customers' and their workers' behavior, raising concerns about workplace manipulation.

Recent elections in the United Kingdom, Germany, the United States, France, and other countries have also prompted concerns about using similar tactics to corrupt democratic political processes.

The use of manipulative tactics online, including dark patterns, has been the cause for widespread concern and dissent. But, in light of the unparalleled capabilities that information technologies and digital media enable, people need to study what manipulation could now look like. What it means to manipulate someone and how one might differentiate events of devious manipulation from other types of power like influence or persuasion has not been fully explored in the new context. It is the same old story: is it manipulation or merely benign persuasion?

This chapter highlights this issue by illustrating a facet of manipulation that utilizes these high-tech tools. We are investigating how information technologies assist manipulative acts and are trying to describe the harm such practices inflict on people and social structures.

We use the phrase "online manipulation" to describe a specific type of manipulative conduct made possible by various digital technologies.

The current digital advertising infrastructure also creates opportunities for political and emotional manipulation. Access to digital surveillance makes it easier to identify people's vulnerabilities and take advantage of them.

- **Surveillance**

  1. Nearly everything people do is tracked, whether they know it or not.
  2. Precisely tailoring advertisements to exploit vulnerabilities is a form of internet manipulation.

- **Digital platforms**

  1. Websites can tailor their content depending on their knowledge of a specific user (Dark Patterns).
  2. They learn as users interact with them.

Why do social media algorithms exist? How do they work?

Social media algorithms make accessing relevant content easier. They also try sifting through less relevant or lower-quality content to eliminate it from the user experience. At the same time, these algorithms are capable of helping brands push their products when they pay for social media advertisements. At its simplest, algorithms automate effort.

Algorithms of social platforms are technological methods of categorizing posts based on relevance rather than publication time, to define which material a user sees first, based on the likelihood that they would actually engage with such information. It is thus a way to automatically create a design to control the user's visual experience.

Algorithms, for example, determine which posts are recommended to you as you go through your Instagram feed or which stories from your friends display first on the dashboard.

They can be created by programmers who employ machine learning. The term "machine learning" refers to how algorithms "understand" how to do tasks under varying levels of human supervision.

Also, algorithms rate and filter data in ways that generate market-like incentives and circumstances of engagement for content creators. Hence, algorithms can automate internet manipulation. So now, malevolent predators needn't even invest time and effort to manipulate their prey. Instead, they can control millions of people over the internet using automated algorithms and dark patterns.

Information processing is a principal function determining the working of algorithms. A recommender-algorithm is a type of algorithm that serves to create different recommendations for the viewer. There are four major approaches to information processing using these algorithms:

1. Content-based

This recommender-algorithm attempts to link a user's profile to particular goods the machine believes the user would enjoy. Individual pieces of material are labeled and classified (often in many ways). Then, when users express interest in a particular tag or category, they are routed to additional items in the same grouping. This is a very common algorithmic tactic.

2. Knowledge-based

This second type of recommender-algorithms is often used on platforms where user behavior is rare or when prior behavior is a poor predictor. Because available data is scarce, these systems rely on users' input to build preferences.

One disadvantage for intermediaries is that knowledge-based and content-based techniques require obtaining and managing a large quantity of information about the products in their catalog. The words "Big Data" ought to come to mind here.

3. Collaborative

This technique, also known as collaborative filtering, solves the need for catalog information by connecting individuals to other users rather than products. Amazon pioneered the strategy of providing suggestions with its well-known "customers who purchased this item also bought" approach.

Collaborative filtering uses the data from many individual profiles to discover similar interests across users and then searches for "missing" things. Notably, the algorithm does not need to understand that these users have a shared interest in a particular genre or artist; it simply examines their behavior for similarities.

Amazon's recommendation systems have had an enormous impact. They have been replicated or adapted by other big platforms such as Netflix and YouTube.

4. Context-aware

Context-awareness is the ability of a system to gather information about its location and use it to modify behavior. As different platforms recognize AI recommendations as a source of value, additional technological developments have transformed the landscape. The increased use of mobile devices has enabled the creation of context-aware suggestions.

Time and IP addresses were already observable when people indulged in online surfing. However, with smartphones and related technological advancements, more sensitive data such as one's exact geographic position can be incorporated in recommender-algorithm system computations.

The nature of feedback commonly used by AI learning agents to update their models and the consequent decisions may steer human users' behavior away from what benefits them. This often happens in a direction that can undermine the individual's autonomy and cause a further disparity between actions and goals, as demonstrated by the addictive and compulsive behavior seen in many social media users. (*Burr et al., 2018*)

Facebook is an excellent example of a user of a very powerful recommender AI system. Your News Feed filters posts, stories, and friends' activities to give you a curated content stream based on the information it has gathered about you. Which content is shown or omitted in the News Feed is determined via a ranking algorithm that Facebook continually tests and develops.

So, IT companies can use the internet to spy on and manipulate us through visual designs meant to trick us, but they can do much more.

One study found that emotions expressed by others on Facebook influence your own emotions via a phenomenon known as emotional contagion. Emotional contagion exists when people transfer positive and negative moods to others.

One experiment manipulated the degree to which people were exposed to emotional expressions in their News Feed. This test was explicitly done to check whether exposure to emotional content resulted in people changing their own posting behaviors to align with what they saw.

Two parallel experiments took place:

- One that reduced exposure to friends' positive emotional content
- One that reduced exposure to friends' negative emotional content

The findings revealed emotional contagion. According to the study, when consumers had positive information removed from their News Feed, a higher percentage of words in people's status updates were negative. When the News Feed reduced the level of negativity shown to the user, a reverse pattern emerged.

These findings imply that the emotions voiced by friends via online social networks influence our own moods, providing the first experimental evidence for large-scale emotional contagion, which seems to be compounded by the prevalence of social media.

Online manipulation campaigns take advantage of more than just advertising. They create deceptive front groups, use fake social media accounts, trick search engine algorithms, and deploy bots to distort online conversations, among other tactics.

The scandal about Cambridge Analytica is more than just a "breach," as Facebook's top management has labeled it. It shows the ability to leverage web data to use algorithms to forecast and affect human behavior in a way that most consumers are unaware of. We are talking about the emotional manipulation of billions of people conducted through one big company. Consider its totality then, with all the billions of people using different social media apps, and perhaps we can comprehend how enormous this phenomenon really is.

Cambridge Analytica captured massive data quantities, approximately fifty million raw profiles. They then utilized big data analytics to generate psycho-graphic profiles to target users with personalized digital adverts and other manipulative content through an intermediate app. Some analysts believe that this vast data-analytics method was utilized to sway political campaigns worldwide.

Finally, it has been proven that the internet certainly plays a role in manipulating individual interests, purchases, and exposure to content, on a global scale. But what about another manipulation done on a similarly large scale? A manipulation perpetrated by something older than the internet? What happens when the media itself begins to skew information to pursue an influence-based agenda?

References:

Adar, E., Tan, D. S., & Teevan, J. (2013, April). Benevolent deception in human computer interaction. In Proceedings of the SIGCHI conference on human factors in computing systems (pp. 1863-1872).

Adjerid, I., Acquisti, A., Brandimarte, L., & Loewenstein, G. (2013, July). Sleights of privacy: Framing, disclosures, and the limits of transparency. In Proceedings of the ninth symposium on usable privacy and security (pp. 1-11)

Aimeur E. Hage H. Amri S. (2018). The Scourge of Online Deception in Social Networks.5th Annual Conf. on Computational Science & Computational Intelligence (CSCI'18), 1266–1271

Arunesh Mathur. 2021. Identifying and Measuring Manipulative User Interfaces at Scale on the Web. Extended Abstracts of the 2021 CHI Conference on Human Factors in Computing Systems. Association for Computing Machinery, New York, NY, USA, Article 7, 1–5.

Balas V.E., Kamolphiwong S., Du KL. (eds) Sentimental Analysis and Deep Learning. Advances in Intelligent Systems and Computing, vol 1408. Springer, Singapore.

Balebako, R., Schaub, F., Adjerid, I., Acquisti, A., & Cranor, L. (2015, October). The impact of timing on the salience of smartphone app privacy notices. In Proceedings of the 5th Annual ACM CCS Workshop on Security and Privacy in Smartphones and Mobile Devices (pp. 63-74).

Bösch,C.,Erb,B.,Kargl,F.,Kopp,H. & Pfattheicher,S.(2016).Tales from the Dark Side: Privacy Dark Strategies and Privacy Dark Patterns. Proceedings on Privacy Enhancing Technologies,2016(4) 237-254.

Brignull, H. (2012). Dark Patterns and Honest Interfaces.

Brignull, H., Brosset, P., Prater, S. V., Wills, M., PenzeyMoog, E., & Greenwood, T. (2011, November 1). Dark patterns: Deception vs. honesty in Ui Design. A-List Apart. Retrieved April 14, 2022, from https://alistapart.com/article/dark-patterns-deception-vs.-honesty-in-ui-design/

Cara, Corina. (2020). DARK PATTERNS IN THE MEDIA: A SYSTEMATIC REVIEW.

Carter S.E. (2021) Is Downloading This App Consistent with My Values?. In: Dennehy D., Griva A., Pouloudi N., Dwivedi Y.K., Pappas I., Mäntymäki M. (eds) Responsible AI and Analytics for an Ethical and Inclusive Digitized Society. I3E 2021. Lecture Notes in Computer Science, vol 12896. Springer, Cham.

Chatila, R., & Havens, J. C. (2019). The IEEE global initiative on ethics of autonomous and intelligent systems. In Robotics and well-being (pp. 11-16). Springer, Cham.

Chowdhury, M. M., & Nygard, K. E. (2017, May). Deception in Cyberspace: An Empirical Study on a Con Man Attack. In 2017 IEEE International Conference on Electro Information Technology (EIT) (pp. 410-415). IEEE.

Conti, G., Sobiesk, E.: Malicious interface design: exploiting the user. In: Proceedings of the 19th International Conference on World Wide Web, pp. 271–280 (2010)

Fitton D., Bell B.T., Read J.C. (2021) Integrating Dark Patterns into the 4Cs of Online Risk in the Context of Young People and Mobile Gaming Apps. In: Ardito C. et al. (eds) Human-Computer Interaction – INTERACT 2021. INTERACT 2021. Lecture Notes in Computer Science, vol 12935. Springer, Cham.

Fritsch, L., (2017). Privacy dark patterns in identity management. In: Fritsch, L., Roßnagel, H. & Hühnlein, D. (Hrsg.), Open Identity Summit 2017. Gesellschaft für Informatik, Bonn. (S. 93-104).

Hossain, M. (2017). Language as the device for psychological manipulation in George Orwell's Nineteen Eighty-Four: a psycholinguistic analysis. European Journal of English Language and Linguistics Research, 5(8), 25-31.

How, J. P. (2018). Ethically aligned design [From the Editor]. IEEE Control Systems Magazine, 38(3), 3-4.

Jamie Luguri, Lior Jacob Strahilevitz, Shining a Light on Dark Patterns, Journal of Legal Analysis, Volume 13, Issue 1, 2021, Pages 43–109

Johanna Gunawan, Amogh Pradeep, David Choffnes, Woodrow Hartzog, and Christo Wilson. 2021. A Comparative Study of Dark Patterns Across Web and Mobile Modalities. Proc. ACM Hum.-Comput. Interact. 5, CSCW2, Article 377 (October 2021), 29 pages.

Karagoel, I., & Nathan-Roberts, D. (2021). Dark Patterns: Social Media, Gaming, and E-Commerce. Proceedings of the Human Factors and Ergonomics Society Annual Meeting, 65(1), 752–756.

Kerstin Bongard-Blanchy, Arianna Rossi, Salvador Rivas, Sophie Doublet, Vincent Koenig, and Gabriele Lenzini. 2021. "I am Definitely Manipulated, Even When I am Aware of it. It's Ridiculous!" - Dark Patterns from the End-User Perspective. Designing Interactive Systems Conference 2021. Association for Computing Machinery, New York, NY, USA, 763–776.

Maier, M., & Harr, R. Dark design patterns: An end-user perspective. Human Technology, 16(2), 170–199.

Mathur, A. (2019, September). Dark Patterns at scale: Findings from a crawl of 11K shopping Websites, 3, No. CSCW, Article 81.

Narayanan, A., Mathur, A., Chetty, M., Kshirsagar, M.: Dark patterns: Past, present, and future: the evolution of tricky user interfaces. Queue 18(2), 67–92 (2020)

New analysis shows how Facebook and Google push users into sharing personal data. Forbrukerrådet. (2018, June 27). Retrieved April 14, 2022, from https://www.forbrukerradet.no/side/facebook-and-google-manipulate-users-into-sharing-personal-data/

Raju S.H., Waris S.F., Adinarayna S., Jadala V.C., Rao G.S. (2022) Smart Dark Pattern Detection: Making Aware of Misleading Patterns Through the Intended App. In: Shakya S.,

Report: Deceived by design. Forbrukerrådet. (2018, June 27). Retrieved April 14, 2022, from https://www.forbrukerradet.no/undersokelse/no-undersokelsekategori/deceived-by-design/

Robert Nord and Zachary Kurtz. (2020, March 16). Using machine learning to detect design patterns. SEI Blog. Retrieved April 14, 2022, from https://insights.sei.cmu.edu/blog/using-machine-learning-to-detect-design-patterns/

Sayan Chaudhry and Chinmay Kulkarni. 2021. Design Patterns of Investing Apps and Their Effects on Investing Behaviors. Designing Interactive Systems Conference 2021. Association for Computing Machinery, New York, NY, USA, 777–788.

Shamsudhin N., Jotterand F. (2021) Social Robots and Dark Patterns: Where Does Persuasion End and Deception Begin?. In: Jotterand F., Ienca M. (eds) Artificial Intelligence in Brain and Mental Health: Philosophical, Ethical & Policy Issues. Advances in Neuroethics. Springer, Cham.

Toth, and Damian Clifford. 2021. Dark Patterns and the Legal Requirements of Consent Banners: An Interaction Criticism Perspective. In Proceedings of the 2021 CHI Conference on Human Factors in Computing Systems (CHI '21).Association for Computing Machinery, New York, NY, USA, Article 172, 1–18.

Willis, L. E. (2020). Deception by design. Harvard Journal of Law & Technology, 34, Number 1 Fall.

Yael Grauer - Jul 28, 2016 12:57 pm U. T. C. (2016, July 28). Dark patterns are designed to trick you (and they're all over the web). Ars Technica. Retrieved April 14, 2022, from https://arstechnica.com/information-technology/2016/07/dark-patterns-are-designed-to-trick-you-and-theyre-all-over-the-web/

Burr, C., Cristianini, N., & Ladyman, J. (2018). An Analysis of the Interaction Between Intelligent Software Agents and Human Users. Minds and machines, 28(4), 735–774. https://doi.org/10.1007/s11023-018-9479-0

Cristianini, N., & Scantamburlo, T. (2019, October 8). On social machines for algorithmic regulation - AI & SOCIETY. SpringerLink; link.springer.com. https://link.springer.com/article/10.1007/s00146-019-00917-8

Nield, D. (2018, August 28). Dark patterns: The ways websites trick us into giving up our privacy. Gizmodo. Retrieved April 14, 2022, from https://gizmodo.com/dark-patterns-how-websites-are-tricking-you-into-givin-1794734134

Key Chapter Eight Takeaways

1. The internet has allowed for the creation of a new type of psychological manipulation called Dark Patterns. This refers to the use of website designs and other visual tools to manipulate the internet user.

2. Dark Patterns are utilized in various ways. Some of the techniques used in Dark Patterns implementation include: Privacy Zuckering, Trick Questions, Sneak-into-basket, Price Comparison Prevention, Hidden Costs, Disguised Ads, Forced Continuity, Friend Spam, Bait-and-Switch, Confirm-Shaming, Misdirection and Roach Motel.

3. Algorithms are used to automate digital manipulation. They are also used to collect massive amounts of data about people. This is called Big Data.

4. Social Media algorithms work to collect data based on four metrics: Content-Based, Knowledge-Based, Collaborative, and Context-Aware patterns.

5. People can be subjected to emotional manipulation on social media by exposing themselves to the positive and negative emotional content of others.

CHAPTER NINE

DECODING MEDIA MANIPULATION

How much do you trust what you see and hear on TV or on the news? People are becoming more disillusioned by many media assertions in the age of "fake news" claims. This is due to the deterioration of media reliability. Many have chosen to stop listening to the news because of this. In line with that, the word media here will henceforth refer to news media.

In the previous chapters, we looked at how governments can be involved in manipulation. We also highlighted how the internet could be used for manipulation. But, governmental manipulation predates the internet, and the original medium of mass manipulation in the modern era is undoubtedly the news media.

Earlier, we looked at how governments in tyrannical regimes oppress the people by suppressing the press. But just like it was mentioned there, a free press is no guarantee of press integrity nor an absence of media manipulation. In fact, "free press" is often a misnomer or mislabel. This idea is the theme of this chapter.

What is the purpose of journalistic media? Like the medical profession, journalism was supposed to have a code of ethics governing it, contributing to its appearance of reliability.

While different codes differ in detail and come from diverse cultural traditions, most share elements such as truthfulness, accuracy, fact-based communications, independence, objectivity, impartiality, fairness, respect for others, and public accountability. These criteria were supposed to be met in the gathering, editing, and dissemination of newsworthy information to the public. (*Global Charter of Ethics for Journalists, 2019*)

That is what ethical journalism looks like and what journalism is supposed to be. The Pulitzer Prize is supposed to reward magnificent achievements in journalism. It is ironically named after Joseph Pulitzer, whose press wars against William Randolph Hearst in the 1890s led to the universal rise of "yellow journalism." News began to focus on advertising revenue and, more importantly, published "news" full of sensationalism, shock, sex, crime, etc.

Why would they do that? To Sell, To Persuade, and To Manipulate. Journalism is supposed to be objective and factual. But these days, many journalists (usually of a particular political affiliation) openly claim journalism should be biased and subjective. (*Schwartz, 2021*)

Additionally, they even claim that this subjectivity is better than being honest and objective. (*Winston & Winston, 2020*). Others argue that subjectivity allows journalists to be skeptics and falsely assert that objectivity cannot meld with skepticism. (*Shapiro, 2021*)

It should then come as no surprise when the latest news analysis conducted by Reuters shows that only 26% of Americans believe that the news is reliable. (*Nielsen et al., Reuters Institute Digital News Report 2022*) The number of people interested in the news has fallen sharply since 2015 too. In the US, this number fell from 67% to 47%. In the UK it dropped from 70% to 43%. (*Nielsen et al., Reuters Institute Digital News Report 2022*)

In Canada, 61% of people actually believed that journalists were lying and trying to mislead them deliberately. (Teo, 2022)

Of course, none of this should imply that news reporters should not become activists. On the contrary, there are several instances where journalists can and should indulge in protests while still doing their duty objectively (*Gilmore, 2014*). However, this requires such journalists to be moral and just. Unfortunately, this is not often the case.

Look at the example of the organization, Poynter. An article on Poynter's website mentioned how objective journalism was a vice of news organizations like the Associated Press. The article even claimed that unbiased reporting was racist, sexist, etc. (*Baleria, 2020*). Unsurprisingly, Poynter is funded by George Soros' Open Society Foundations, while All Sides rates Associated Press as one of the most unbiased news networks in the country. (*All Sides, 2022*)

Media manipulation is real, and many news organizations are corrupt and biased. Opinionated news has been used to target consumers' emotions and manipulate their behavior. These news organizations have now begun to do so more vociferously and vehemently because of the power offered by the internet and social media.

The aim of using the news-media vehicle to influence on a broader scale is to control the people who consume it. Before the growth of the blog and the web-driven media cycle, media manipulation was often relegated to government propaganda and agenda-driven publicists with specific aims. (*Barro, 2004*). These tactics exploited the public trust in the media for their own gains. Now that trust may not be as strong, but the potential for exaggeration and fabrication is higher than ever. (*Bradshaw et al., 2021*)

Media manipulation exploits people by creating a difference between perception and reality. (*Holiday, 2012*) The similarities with gaslighting are undeniable. In mass media, this manipulation typically involves a collection of strategies in which partisan interests generate an impression that benefits their specific interests.

Such strategies may feature logical fallacies, deception, disinformation, manipulation, propaganda, and rhetorical techniques. These are frequently used to hide information or viewpoints by inducing people to stop paying attention to specific arguments or to deflect their attention elsewhere.

In reality, media disinformation is now an industrialized practice performed on a massive, global scale. Some of the more common forms of media manipulation are discussed below.

Propaganda

As explained previously, propaganda is a form of communication generally used to further an agenda that might or might not be based on truth. It may include selectively presented facts to influence a viewpoint or use loaded language to elicit an emotional response instead of a rational response to the given information. (*Bradshaw et al., 2021*)

Propaganda is frequently associated with material prepared by government agencies as part of political campaigns, war efforts, health campaigns, large corporations, revolutionaries, extra-religious organizations, and the media. Propaganda is the most common kind of media manipulation. In fact, government or state propaganda is disseminated using news media more than any other vehicle. (*Weaver, 1994*)

In such a scenario, the people cannot be blamed for thinking that the news is inaccurate. (*Vanderwicken, 1995*). On the contrary, it is a valid, logical reaction to the awareness that media manipulation is confirmed. When disinformation is industrialized, dogmatic belief in "news" organizations may be just what the media wants. But it certainly should not be what citizens think because dogma is used to manipulate them. (*Media Manipulation & Disinformation, 2021*)

Smear tactics

A smear campaign is a deliberate, calculated attempt designed to harm a person or group's image, credibility, and reputation. This is also called character assassination. Smear campaigns, like negative campaigning, frequently target government officials, lawmakers, political candidates, and other prominent personalities.

In this case, the media becomes a weapon that can be used to destroy one's opponents. This weapon can be quite potent and is potentially as ruinous as the cancel culture employed in social media.

Private individuals or groups may become victims of smear campaigns carried out in corporations, institutions, the judicial system, and other formal entities. Discrediting strategies such as releasing disparaging remarks are intended to dissuade others from trusting in the individual or backing their cause. These usually comprise of inadvertent comments made by the individual ages ago, things taken out of context, or may even include fabricated claims.

Smear tactics are distinct from regular dialogue or discussion in that they have no bearing on the topics or arguments at hand. Instead, a smear is a straightforward attempt to discredit a group or individual to undermine their credibility.

Fake news

Fake news is incorrect or misleading information that is presented as news. Fake news is frequently used to harm a person or entity's reputation or profit from advertising income. Although false news has existed throughout history, the phrase "fake news" was coined in the 1890s when dramatic newspaper stories were widespread.

However, the phrase has often been misused with no clear meaning. It has been used more generally to cover any sort of misleading information, including inadvertent and unconscious falsehoods. Many people use this term, including high-profile individuals who refer to any news that is opposed to their own opinions as fake news. The "fake news" label can be used as an artifice tool. That's ironic.

Hyper partisan news outlets

Media sites that deviate from typical conceptions of impartiality in journalism are transgressors, blatantly ideological, and severely prejudiced. When the objectivity expected of journalists is undermined, it is no surprise that this objectivity is lost in media organizations too.

In the last ten years, a vast, allegedly partisan system of right-wing news websites and blogs has taken root. While the American right has a long history of using new media, dating back to anti-communist radio networks, the present network extends beyond that. Breitbart is supposedly at the heart of this new market, as are sites such as The Daily Caller, The Washington Examiner, The Gateway Pundit, Infowars, Truthfeed, and Conservative Treehouse. (*Barthel et al., 2016*)

These right-wing outlets can be considered a response to the deliberate left-wing tilt many legacy media outlets openly display. The New York Times, The Washington Post, Huffington Post, Vanity Fair, The Guardian, Newsweek, Time Magazine, CBS, NBC, CNN, etc., are all hyper-partisan in their leftist stances. (*All Sides, 2022*). This has been evidenced in their agenda-driven programming. There is thus undisputed media manipulation across all political aisles. (*Anderson & Rainie, 2017*)

Although Fox News appears conservative, it is not nearly as far to the right as many major news outlets are to the political left, and they have been this way for a very long time. (*Barro, 2004*)

This divisive, agenda-driven, manipulative news-making has created a similar divide among consumers. Conservative people distrust leftist media, while leftists pay little heed to Fox News and other right-leaning news outlets. (*Mitchell et al., 2020*). This polarization is one of the primary adverse outcomes of media manipulation.

This problem is not exclusive to the USA. Media Manipulation exists in just about every country that has media. (*Nielsen et al., Reuters Institute Digital News Report 2022*) In India, words like "Godi Media" has been created to represent media organizations that are perceived to be nothing but mouthpieces of the ruling government. The word Godi Media literally means Media sitting in the lap [of the government].

In 2018, on World Press Freedom Day, several protests happened against the existence of such media manipulation. However, this trend continues, and the situation has worsened, with India now being ranked at its lowest rank of 150 in the 2022 World Press Freedom Report. (*NL Team, 2022*) Many elements of the Indian media are now called lapdogs instead of watchdogs.

News consumption has been steadily declining since the 2010s began. Every year, more and more people assert that they distrust the media and find news organizations unreliable. (*Nielsen et al., Reuters Institute Digital News Report 2022*)

Despite this global distrust, news organizations saw a jump in monthly subscriptions and revenue increase during the Covid lockdowns. This spike has only added to the general public's suspicions about news media.

The percentage of people who reported believing that the media was corrupt and untrustworthy varied across countries. It was 72% in Kenya and Nigeria, 31% in Germany, 46% in the UK, 54% in Brazil, etc. (*Nielsen et al., Reuters Institute Digital News Report 2022*)

To summarize this politicization aspect, media manipulation follows the media bias prevailing in each media organization. In other words, leftist media will indulge in manipulation to further leftist causes and vice versa.

Media manipulation and social media

Okay, so we mentioned how disinformation is now industrialized, but what does that mean? In the contemporary world, industrialized dissemination of disinformation can be done most effectively when social media is used. According to the Oxford Internet Institute's (OII) 2020 media manipulation survey, which found evidence of corruption in all 80-plus countries surveyed, social media manipulation of public opinion is a growing threat to democracies worldwide.

Organized social media manipulation campaigns were discovered in all eighty-one countries surveyed. The report showed that governments, public relations firms, and political parties generate disinformation on a vast scale. Furthermore, it demonstrated that disinformation had become a common occurrence. It was used as part of political communication in more than ninety-three percent of the countries surveyed (76 out of 81)!!

The OII team warns that social media manipulation has increased, with governments and political parties spending millions on private-sector "cyber troops" who drown out other voices on social media. In addition, citizen influencers are being used to disseminate manipulative messages. These include volunteers, youth groups, and civil society organizations that support the ideologies of the manipulators. Artificial intelligence in the form of bots is also used to manipulate people through false messages and false social proof.

The report says that government agencies, political parties, and private firms continue to use social media to spread political propaganda. They are polluting the digital information ecosystem and suppressing freedom of speech and the press. A significant portion of this activity has become professionalized, with private firms providing disinformation-for-hire services.

The following are some of the key findings identified by the OII researchers:

- Researchers have identified state actors working with private "strategic communications" firms in forty-eight countries. They are playing an increasing role in spreading propaganda on a massive scale.
- In 2022 alone, almost $60 million has been spent on companies that use bots and other amplification strategies to create the appearance of trending political messaging.
- Cyber troops are frequently linked directly to state agencies. In sixty-two countries, they found evidence of a government agency using digital propaganda to shape public attitudes.
- According to Oxford researchers, established political parties also use social media to "spread disinformation, suppress political participation, and undermine opposition parties."

The report delves into the tools and techniques of internet-based propaganda, such as using fake accounts, bots, humans, and hacked accounts, to disseminate disinformation. It discovered:

Human accounts were used by seventy-nine countries, bot accounts by fifty-seven countries, and hacked or stolen accounts by fourteen countries. In addition, researchers investigated how cyber troops control public opinion through various communication strategies such as disinformation or manipulated media, data-driven targeting, and abusive tactics such as mounting smear campaigns or online harassment.

The results were similar to the apocalyptic world of the novel 1984. Millions of people around the globe were being manipulated regularly to act against their best interests.

During the scandal that arose over the elimination of journalist Jamal Kashoggi, it came to light how a Middle Eastern government had an enormous team of people dedicated to spreading social media disinformation.

According to the report, seventy-six countries used disinformation and media manipulation as part of their campaigns in 2019, up from forty-seven countries in 2019. Thirty countries used data-driven strategies to target specific users with political advertisements. Fifty-nine countries used state-sponsored trolls to attack political opponents or activists in 2019.

So far, we have explored the most contemporary forms of media manipulation. However, understanding media manipulation cannot be achieved in isolation. First, one must understand the context in which media manipulation takes place. We must explore the background of media manipulation. Who is manipulating the media? Who stands behind the propaganda? Fortunately, we have had a hundred years of prodigious research examining this phenomenon.

Politico-media complex

The root of media manipulation lies in a concept called the politico-media complex (PMC), which is the interconnected network of the government, the "ruling elite," and the media industry. The PMC is analogous to the military-industrial complex concept.

From the invention of the Gutenberg Press to the heyday of the Print Media in the last century, newspapers became the greatest arbiter of information. Press barons became the most powerful men in their countries. The "Fourth Estate" became another vehicle for controlling the masses. People came to know about the world through news articles and editorial opinions. As such, the owners of news organizations became instrumental in governmental functioning.

The invention of the radio added to the power of news sources. Print media still reigned supreme, but the development of television revolutionized news delivery. As a result, print media soon began to lose its importance compared to visual news media. Today, even the most influential newspapers have shifted their focus to digital media. Online news sites are the primary vehicles of information.

A news organization is like any other business where operating costs and the profit motive are concerned. From the Pulitzer-Hearst battles of the 1890s came the rise of sensationalist news. Now sensationalism merged with governmental messaging to create the complex machinery whose output we call propaganda.

A hundred years ago, in 1922, Walter Lippman published the book Public Opinion, followed by the Phantom Public. His protégé, Edward Bernays, then released Propaganda in 1928, followed by Public Relations in 1945. Today Bernays is called the "Father of Spin." These seminal books provided stellar insights into how the media worked as an excellent vehicle for manipulating the public.

But why? Why does media manipulation occur, and what drives it?

Vox populi

The "voice of the people" in Latin, but used in English to refer to the "opinion of the majority," vox populi is the foundation of a democratic process. It works on the assumption that all men are created equal, further presuming that all ideas are equal. Democracy then should always choose ideas supported by the majority of a population: in essence, quantity over quality.

Most of the educated world knows about the concept of individual sovereignty. It is closely connected with individual liberty and accountability. There is also a concept called popular sovereignty. This is defined as the principle whereby the authority of a political entity and its associated government are made and maintained by the consent of its people.

In an indirect democracy, this popular sovereignty is exercised by the people's elected representatives. This is usually how most national and other central governments of democratic countries work today, or rather it is how they are supposed to work. Benjamin Franklin applied this concept when he proposed that, in free countries, the rulers are the servants while the people are their superiors and rulers.

It is a noble idea, but the reality is different. Democratic function depends on the people's consent if the process is conducted legitimately, honestly, and genuinely. This is how elections are supposed to work: to elect representatives who are then authorized to use this democratic power.

However, this vox populi, this consent, is not unassailable. In authoritarian regimes, the tyrant/s can exercise power by diktat: rule as they wish. In democracies, the powers that be, depend on this idea of "consent." A country's citizens can only properly contribute to popular sovereignty if they have informed consent.

Informed consent refers to the choices made by a knowledgeable populace. If the voting public remains uninformed, their support is typically engineered (*Bernays et al., 1955*) or manufactured. (*Herman & Chomsky, 1988*)

The words above are tributes to the masterful scholars Edward Bernays, Edward Herman, and the famous Noam Chomsky. Their work has helped us understand how the "consent" of the common public and the choices made by the public are subjected to the control of others through media manipulation.

And that is the most common reason for media manipulation. The desire to control what the common public thinks, chooses, and acts.

How did media manipulation get worse?

Freedom of speech and expression, one of the most fundamental rights in the world today, is often closely connected to the concept of a free press. Interestingly, the impetus for the beginning of the American War for Independence and thus for all modern democracies includes a book that is proportionally one of the best-selling American books of all time.

This book was written by a man who immigrated to the 13 American colonies with the help of Benjamin Franklin himself. The book, aptly titled Common Sense, is authored by Thomas Paine. During the American Revolution, Common Sense was attacked by many who said that without a monarchy, the government would "degenerate into democracy".

The Founders of the US gave its citizens several legal protections in the form of rights. These protections include the concept of a free press. This can be easily understood using an analogy. Slavery is the ownership of one human being by another. By definition, a slave is not free. It is then logical to posit that anything owned cannot be completely free. This became the problem at the foundation of the news media industry.

There is a reason why journalism, through the idea of a free press, is the only profession directly protected in the US Constitution; Congress shall make no law abridging the freedom of the press. The press was and is expected to help the public hold the government accountable and prevent the evil abuse of power. So, the government cannot overly or overtly hinder or limit the press. They cannot "own" the press.

But others can. One of the first measures of the nascent US was to encourage the formation of independent press organizations through the use of subsidies. During this period, the subsidies did not depend on or discriminate against the newspaper's content, or at least they were not supposed to.

As time went on, the operating costs of newspaper publishers grew. Most of their revenue came not from the sales of newspapers but from advertisements in the newspapers.

Soon, corporate ownership of press companies grew. Profit became the driving force behind news publishing. There is, of course, nothing inherently wrong with that. One can even argue that it is good if free-market capitalism works unhindered. But in the news sphere, which is the lifeblood of a democracy, making the press work as mediums-for-profit above everything else, was a recipe for catastrophe for the common man.

The crony capitalism that followed corporate ownership of the press led to massive media consolidation, just as in other industries. The Politico-Media Complex now became a nexus of power with three vertices. The Media Companies, the Government, and the Corporations whose money funded the media companies' functioning were the three power centers. The enormous conflicts of interests that can and did follow such a system should come as no surprise. It is that blatantly obvious.

Mass media used to make over 236 billion dollars in advertising revenue, and that was before 2012. With the explosion of social media, that figure is now near 750 billion dollars, a 300 percent growth in a single decade. Similarly, studies have postulated that about forty to seventy percent of news content comes from some corporate PR department. Since the 1980s, there has been plenty of consolidations and mergers. There has also been the explosive rise of IT companies, which has created an enormous issue of crony capitalism in the media industry.

Noam Chomsky's book, Manufacturing Consent, was written in the 1980s in response to the alarming state of media monopoly when just fifty companies controlled ninety percent of the media. The situation was considered critical and caused widespread concern. In 2011, ninety percent was owned by just six companies! That's right.

Seven corporations owned over a hundred broadcast and cable networks in 2011: Fox Corporation, The Walt Disney Company (which owns the ABC, ESPN, FX, and Disney brands), National Amusements (which owns Paramount Global), Comcast (which owns NBCUniversal), Warner Bros. Discovery, E. W. Scripps Company, Cablevision (now known as Altice USA), or some combination thereof. (*Lutz, 2012*)

This state of affairs shows that mighty corporate conglomerates hold enormous power within news media. This is not unique to the media industry, but the concerns it raises are uniquely dangerous. It's where media manipulation comes in. Financial or profit considerations can persuade news media to mold public opinion how they see fit. Government clout in news media can do the same.

This has led to the vehement public distrust of mass media that we discussed earlier. According to Gallup, in 2012, sixty percent of the American public had little trust in the news media concerning honest reporting. The 2020 Gallup poll showed that seventy-three percent distrusted the media. So, both Gallup and Reuters have found growing public distrust of the News Media.

After the Freedom Convoy protests, trust in the news media fell to 42% in Canada. This still makes Canada one of the countries with the highest confidence in media. (*Nielsen et al., Reuters Institute Digital News Report 2022*)

In 2020 in the US, only nine percent trusted the news media. Let us reconsider that. Nine percent of the American population trusted the one profession protected by the US Constitution; an industry set up to protect citizens from government abuse and tyranny.

Along with the distrust, it has been speculated that the American political establishment has gained considerable power over the years. Unfortunately, this gain has coincided with an associated "dumbing down" of the populace. (*Shenkman, 2008*). This colossal insult to the common public is a direct result of the media manipulation of the last few decades. (*Mosley, 2000*). This is how it works. Media manipulation leads to public distrust, which leads to a less informed public, and that leads to greater power for the state.

Let us briefly consider situations where media manipulation has played a considerable role. The infamous Nike-Vietnam abuse scandal of the 1990s and the notorious 1996 Trans World Airlines Flight 800 incident are two instances where corporate interests and governmental interests were alleged to have deplorably destroyed journalistic integrity and manipulated public attention away from the real story. (*Tremblay, 2012*)

The crack epidemic and the War on Drugs are already quite well known. Perhaps today, what is not as well known is the Nicaraguan cocaine pipeline and the resulting media scandal that eventually led to the alleged suicide of the Dark Alliance series reporter, Pulitzer-Prize winning story writer, Gary Webb. (*Tremblay, 2012*)

There are numerous other instances where media spin and silence have been used to manipulate the public. These include, among others East Timor, Cambodia reporting problems of the 1970s and the "Smoking Gun" problem of the 2000s, etc. (*Tremblay, 2012*)

If only the effect of media manipulation stopped at the borders of distant countries.

Finally - What's the WORST hazard of media manipulation?

Yes, it is not a trick question or a rhetorical one. Media manipulation has led to the "dumbing down" of the public, its loss of popular sovereignty, and an even more significant loss of individual sovereignty and liberty. And yet, none of those is the worst problem to stem from media manipulation. That tag would have to be the agenda-setting and cultural assault caused by media manipulation.

The author of Manufacturing Consent, one of the most famous intellectuals, has always been quite close to some politically leftist ideals. When he wrote about the inherent problems of media consolidation and 'real' capitalism, it appeared incorrect and false. Real capitalism or free-market capitalism cannot be both an inherent problem and a great vehicle to combat poverty simultaneously.

However, in 2001, during an interview, Chomsky corrected and clarified his stance based on the development of another 1967 paper he wrote. I was of the same opinion before knowing about this 2001 interview. The problem is not corporate ownership per se. It is the ideological bent of the intellectual culture prevailing at a time when mass media is used for manipulation. In other words, media manipulation is a tool.

Agenda-setting theory explains how mass media can manipulate the public and affect the importance of specific topics. (*McCombs & Reynolds, 2002*) When connected with the intellectual culture prevailing in the power centers at a given time, this can affect the culture of the ordinary people of a country. One example is the crisis created by the reality-distorting, pseudo-scientific offshoots of critical theory.

This agenda-setting and cultural assault are made worse by the "culture of lying" that prevails in some sections of news media. (*Weaver, 1994*). The public's culture determines their way of life, aspirations, values, etc. Media manipulation can destroy this quite quickly. It has happened before, and it is happening now too.

In the next chapter, we shall look more closely at the kind of manipulation that stems from the profit-driven motivation of business organizations. After all, their ownership of media has contributed to the worsening of media manipulation. It makes sense then to look at what other kinds of manipulation these business concerns get involved in.

References:

A Reckoning Over Objectivity, Led by Black Journalists. (2020, June 23). The New York Times | Opinion; www.nytimes.com. https://www.nytimes.com/2020/06/23/opinion/objectivity-black-journalists-coronavirus.html

AllSides Media Bias Ratings. AllSides; www.allsides.com. Retrieved May 5, 2022, from https://www.allsides.com/media-bias/ratings

Anderson, J., & Rainie, L. (2017, October 19). The Future of Truth and Misinformation Online | Pew Research Center. Pew Research Center: Internet, Science & Tech; www.pewresearch.org. https://www.pewresearch.org/internet/2017/10/19/the-future-of-truth-and-misinformation-online/

Bagdikian, B. H. (1983). The Media Monopoly. Beacon Press.

Baleria, G. (2020, September 11). It's time for journalism educators to rethink "objectivity" and teach more about context. Poynter; www.poynter.org. https://www.poynter.org/educators-students/2020/its-time-for-journalism-educators-to-rethink-objectivity-and-teach-more-about-context/

Barro, R. J. (2004, June 14). The Liberal Media: It's No Myth. Harvard Scholar. https://scholar.harvard.edu/barro/files/04_0614_liberalmedia_bw.pdf

Barthel, M., Mitchell, A., & Holcomb, J. (2016, December 15). Many Americans Believe Fake News Is Sowing Confusion. Pew Research Center's Journalism Project; www.pewresearch.org. https://www.pewresearch.org/journalism/2016/12/15/many-americans-believe-fake-news-is-sowing-confusion/

Bernays, E. (1928). Propaganda. Routledge. https://doi.org/10.1604/9780970312594

Bernays, E. (1945). Public Relations. Bellman. https://doi.org/10.1604/9781419173387

Bernays, E. L., Cutler, H. W., Dodge, S., Samstag, N., Fleischman, D., Jones, J. P., Fine, B., & Ginsburgh, R. A. (1955). The Engineering of Consent. University of Oklahoma Press. https://doi.org/10.1604/9780806103280

Bradshaw, S., Bailey, H., & Howard, P. N. (2021, January 13). Industrialized Disinformation: 2020 Global Inventory of Organized Social Media Manipulation. Oxford Internet Institute. https://demtech.oii.ox.ac.uk/research/posts/industrialized-disinformation/

Chomsky, N. (1989). Necessary Illusions: Thought Control in Democratic Societies. South End Press.

Coleman, G. (2016) Hacker. In Peters, B. (Ed.), *Digital keywords: a vocabulary of information society and culture*. Princeton University Press.

Conklin, Michael, The Overlooked Benefits of 'Hate Speech': Not Just the Lesser of Two Evils (2020). http://dx.doi.org/10.2139/ssrn.3604244

Cunningham, B. (2003, July 1). Re-thinking Objectivity. Columbia Journalism Review; archives.cjr.org. https://archives.cjr.org/feature/rethinking_objectivity.php

Gilmore, D. (2014, December 2). When Journalists Must Not Be Objective. Wired; www.wired.com. https://www.wired.com/2014/12/when-journalists-must-not-be-objective/

Global Charter of Ethics for Journalists. (2019, June 12). IFJ; www.ifj.org. https://www.ifj.org/who/rules-and-policy/global-charter-of-ethics-for-journalists.html

Herman, E. S., & Chomsky, N. (1988). Manufacturing Consent. Pantheon. https://doi.org/10.1604/9780679720348

Herman, Edward S., & Chomsky, Noam. (2002). Manufacturing consent : the political economy of the mass media. New York: Pantheon Books.

Holiday, R. (2012, July 16). What is Media Manipulation?--A Definition and Explanation. Forbes; www.forbes.com. https://www.forbes.com/sites/ryanholiday/2012/07/16/what-is-media-manipulation-a-definition-and-explanation/?sh=198725f43939

Holiday, R. (2013). Trust Me, I'm Lying: Confessions of a Media Manipulator. Portfolio.

Howard, Jeffrey. (2019). Free Speech and Hate Speech. Annual Review of Political Science. 22. 93-109. 10.1146/annurev-polisci-051517-012343.

Kennedy, Brendan & Atari, Mohammad & Mostafazadeh Davani, Aida & Yeh, Leigh & Omrani, Ali & Kim, Yehsong & Coombs, Kristopher & Havaldar, Shreya & Portillo-Wightman, G J & Gonzalez, Elaine

& Hoover, Joe & Azatian, Aida & Hussain, Alyzeh & Lara, Austin & Cardenas, Gabriel & Omary, Adam & Park, Christina & Wang, Xin & Wijaya, Clarisa & Dehghani, Morteza. (2022). Introducing the Gab Hate Corpus: defining and applying hate-based rhetoric to social media posts at scale. Language Resources and Evaluation. 56. 1-30. 10.1007/s10579-021-09569-x

Lippman, W. (1922). Public Opinion. Harcourt, Brace & Co.

Lippmann, W. (1925). The Phantom Public. Transaction Publishers. https://doi.org/10.1604/9781560006770

Lutz, A. (2012, June 14). These 6 Corporations Control 90% of the Media in America. Business Insider; www.businessinsider.com. https://www.businessinsider.com/these-6-corporations-control-90-of-the-media-in-america-2012-6?IR=T

McCombs, M. (2005). A Look at Agenda-setting: past, present and future. Journalism Studies; www.tandfonline.com. https://www.tandfonline.com/doi/abs/10.1080/14616700500250438

McCombs, M., & Reynolds, A. (2002). News influence on our pictures of the world. In J. Bryant & D. Zillmann (Eds.), Media effects: Advances in theory and research (pp. 1–18). Lawrence Erlbaum Associates Publishers. https://psycnet.apa.org/record/2002-00742-001

Media Manipulation & Disinformation. (2021, February 1). Data & Society; datasociety.net. https://datasociety.net/research/media-manipulation/

Media Manipulation. (2006, April 17). Global Issues; www.globalissues.org. https://www.globalissues.org/article/532/media-manipulation

Mitchell, A., Gottfried, J., Kiley, J., & Matsa, K. E. (2020, August 28). Section 1: Media sources: Distinct favorites emerge on the left and right. Pew Research Center's Journalism Project. Retrieved April 14, 2022, from https://www.pewresearch.org/journalism/2014/10/21/section-1-media-sources-distinct-favorites-emerge-on-the-left-and-right/

Mosley, I. (2000). Dumbing Down. Imprint Academic. https://doi.org/10.1604/9780907845652

Nielsen, R. K., Newman, N., Fletcher, R., Robertson, C. T., & Eddy, K. (2022, June 1). Reuters Institute Digital News Report 2022. Reuters Institute For The Study Of Journalism. Retrieved June 19, 2022, from https://reutersinstitute.politics.ox.ac.uk/sites/default/files/2022-06/Digital_News-Report_2022.pdf

Nunez, M. (2016, May 9). Former Facebook Workers: We Routinely Suppressed Conservative News. Gizmodo; gizmodo.com. https://gizmodo.com/former-facebook-workers-we-routinely-suppressed-conser-1775461006

Research guides. Research Guides. (n.d.). Retrieved April 14, 2022, from https://guides.lib.umich.edu/fakenews

Schwartz, M. (2021, April 14). True journalism can't be objective. Massachusetts Daily Collegian; dailycollegian.com. https://dailycollegian.com/2021/04/true-journalism-cant-be-objective/

Shapiro, I. (2021, April 8). UNWANTED QUESTIONS: Skepticism, not objectivity, is what makes journalism matter. Ryerson University Centre for Free Expression; cfe.ryerson.ca. https://cfe.ryerson.ca/blog/2021/04/unwanted-questions-skepticism-not-objectivity-what-makes-journalism-matter

Shenkman, R. (2008). Just How Stupid Are We? Facing the Truth about the American Voter. Basic Books. https://doi.org/10.1604/9780465077717

Taflinger, R. F. (1996, May 29). The Myth of Objectivity in Journalism. Washington State University; public.wsu.edu. https://public.wsu.edu/~taflingc/mythobj.html

Tanner Mirrlees. 2021. GAFAM and Hate Content Moderation: Deplatforming and Deleting the Alt-right. Media and Law: Between Free Speech and Censorship, 81-97.

Team, N.L. (2022, May 3). World Press Freedom Index 2022: India's rank falls from 142 to 150, press freedom is "in crisis." News Laundry; www.newslaundry.com. https://www.newslaundry.com/2022/05/03/world-press-freedom-index-2022-indias-rank-falls-from-142-to-150-press-freedom-is-in-crisis

Teo, I. (2022, June 18). Canadians Increasingly Losing Trust in Media, Study Finds. Www.Theepochtimes.Com; www.theepochtimes.com. https://www.theepochtimes.com/canadians-increasingly-losing-trust-in-media-avoiding-news-that-fatigue-them-study-finds_4542333.html

Thaler, R. H., & Sunstein, C. R. (2009). Nudge: Improving Decisions about Health, Wealth, and Happiness. Penguin Books. https://doi.org/10.1604/9780143115267

The lost meaning of Objectivity. (2022, May). American Press Institute; www.americanpressinstitute.org. https://www.americanpressinstitute.org/journalism-essentials/bias-objectivity/lost-meaning-objectivity/

van Dijck, J. (2014). Datafication, dataism and dataveillance: Big Data between scientific paradigm and ideology. *Surveillance & Society*, *12*(2), 197–208.

Vanderwicken, P. (1995, May 1). Why the News Is Not the Truth. Harvard Business Review; hbr.org. https://hbr.org/1995/05/why-the-news-is-not-the-truth

Weaver, P. (1994). News and the Culture of Lying. Free Press. https://doi.org/10.1604/9780029340219

Winston, B., & Winston, M. (2020). The Roots of Fake News: Objecting to Objective Journalism. Routledge.

Yang, X., Chen, BC., Maity, M., Ferrara, E. (2016). Social Politics: Agenda Setting and Political Communication on Social Media. In: Spiro, E., Ahn, YY. (eds) Social Informatics. SocInfo 2016. Lecture Notes in Computer Science(), vol 10046. Springer, Cham. https://doi.org/10.1007/978-3-319-47880-7_20

Key Chapter Nine Takeaways

1. Media manipulation refers to media organizations exploiting people by distorting perspectives of reality.

2. Malevolent actors often use media companies to spread mass disinformation to target consumers and mold them psychologically.

3. Many journalists have begun to reject ethics and objectivity in pursuit of their radical activism and political agendas. The typical trustworthiness attached to the journalism profession allows people to be manipulated by opinionated journalism.

4. Hyper-partisan news outlets on both sides of the political spectrum have begun to polarize the country.

5. Disinformation, propaganda, smear tactics, and fake news have grown on an industrial scale.

6. Social media plays a massive role in media manipulation. It has been found that the government-media nexus has spent a vast amount of resources on mass manipulation using social media.

7. Media manipulation tools include both human beings and algorithms.

8. The Politico-Media Complex is one of the primary media manipulators, and this nexus uses its power to pursue its interests at the expense of the public. It comprises the government, media companies, and corporate companies.

9. The Vox Populi, or the voice of the public and its iteration, is one of the main targets of media manipulation. Manufactured/Engineered consent describes this kind of mass media manipulation.

10. Media manipulation gets worse with the widespread consolidation of news media companies and even cross-industry mergers. Less than ten corporations control over ninety percent of media companies. Profit dictates how news media are run, which easily distorts honest reporting.

11. Media manipulation has led to the political establishment gaining power at the expense of the public, which has suffered a "dumbing down" effect.

12. The worst crisis caused by media manipulation is the agenda-setting effect that strikes at the general population's values and tries to spread the opposing pseudo-intellectual culture of a minority determined to destroy the way of life of an entire nation.

CHAPTER TEN

ADDRESSING ADVERTISING
MANIPULATION

I wonder if there is some random glacier in Antarctica that has not been targeted by ads yet. It is unlikely. On a serious note, consumerism and corporatism have become such massive components of daily life in the civilized world that it is almost inconceivable to live even a single day without seeing an advertisement.

By their very nature, advertisements and marketing strategies are designed to influence consumers. Companies want their products to be purchased, so they spend millions of dollars each year determining how they can best convert potential consumers into actual customers. This chapter describes advertising manipulation and what it looks like and provides key examples.

When you think of advertising manipulation, you may not be thinking of the laundry detergent commercial you just watched or the ad for a real-estate company you saw in the newspaper the other day. Instead, what first comes to mind is probably the idea of "false advertising."

Manipulation via advertising has become an issue that most people face daily. This phenomenon shifts marketing's aim away from satisfying consumers' wants. It expands the power disparities between the corporation and the consumer. It is yet another example of the power imbalance theme we have explored.

It is hard to establish the manipulative nature of every commercial out there. Still, it is possible to focus on the general principles of advertising. We will also try to uncover the psychological manipulation utilized by sellers in different scenarios as they try to encourage people to part with their money.

The ultimate purpose of advertising is to convince consumers to buy a service or product. Manipulative advertising tries to do this by employing facts and reasoning to play on customers' emotions.

The most common devices employed in advertising manipulation include exaggeration of product quality, scarcity, exclusivity, faulty argumentation, and emotional appeals. These are used through the following processes.

1. Target pain and pleasure points: Organizations target their customers' pain and pleasure points. This targeting is only possible through prodigious research and study. Companies have successfully gotten to know their customers as intimately as possible. Once again, it is quite clear that knowledge is key to creating the power imbalance between consumers and corporations (targets and manipulators, respectively).

2. Sell them the dream: Organizations do not show them what can be done; they show them what life can be after procuring the product or service. This is reminiscent of an age-old concept famous in Indian philosophy that says the goal is important and not the means to achieve it. This is precisely what the advertisers do when they discard ethics in the pursuit of profit.

They also make ads that focus on the dream outcomes their products or services will allegedly provide their customers. However, they seldom show the means or methods by which the dream will be accomplished. This is yet another case of appealing to emotions while preventing the consumers from thinking logically.

3. Reuse successful concepts: These organizations will continue with the same narrative until it becomes tired and a new one is required. They once again rely on the fact that people rarely purchase using logical reasoning. This illogical purchasing behavior seen in most people is exactly why we should resist this form of manipulation.

In today's world, we are dealing less with blatant false advertising and more with advertisements that have been designed to encourage certain behaviors in consumers: in other words, psychological manipulation.

Common persuasive techniques used in advertising

Most frequent persuasion techniques employed in dark-psychological advertising include:

1. Association: This is a very effective strategy. It seeks to connect a service or product with something the target client already likes, such as pleasure, security, beauty, fun, or money. It has the potential to elicit a robust emotional response.

2. Beautiful people: A common advertisement technique is one that implies that the buyers will look exactly like the beautiful people in the ads if they use the offered product.

3. Warm and fuzzy: This type features videos or images of families, animals, and children designed to initiate feelings of pleasure, joy, comfort, and warmth.

4. Nostalgia: Nostalgia features a "golden time" when quality was better and life simpler. Nostalgia is a very powerful device and has been recognized in the study of rhetoric for thousands of years. This works on the emotional strength of the consumers' memories of times gone by.

5. Intensity and weasel words: These methods grab potential buyers' attention with emotion-intensifying words like superlatives, hyperbolic claims, and comparatives.

- Superlatives – most, greatest, best, fastest, lowest prices, etc.
- Comparatives – improved, more, better, less fat, healthier, etc.
- Hyperbolic claims – terrific, amazing, tremendous, etc.

6. Celebrity endorsement: Advertisers will also use celebrities to capture our attention. Celebrities promote products/services in advertisements. Companies pay celebrities a lot of money to advertise a product, and this form of testimonial appears effective since many people are in awe of superstars.

Celebrity culture is the modern equivalent of a powerful argument from an authority, which is obviously foolish because the celebrity's endorsement is worthless in terms of objective truth. A scientist's view on science is not the same as a celebrity's view on science in terms of inherent authority. Yet, millions of people succumb to this manipulation device.

7. Plain folks' technique: The reverse of using a celebrity in an advertisement is using ordinary people. This strategy works because many people are likelier to believe an ordinary person than a well-paid superstar. This method is more commonly used for regular items, such as cleansers or cleaning powder.

This is an example of an appeal to identity — a situation where other people of the same type supposedly share the ordinary person's characteristics. Appeal to identity is a different use of authority; the idea is that if someone like you believes this opinion, it must be true. This is an example of the social proof concept discussed in the Persuasion Chapter.

8. Flattery: Marketers and advertisers impress or flatter their target audiences by stating things like "you earned it", "you need more," or "you need only the best." This is yet another type of appeal to emotions. People who like being praised and complimented often fall for this device.

9. Bribery: This strategy attempts to entice people to purchase a product or service by offering something else, like a discount, gift voucher, or rebate. Buyers are familiar with sales, special offers, sweepstakes, and contests. We've all heard of the "buy one, get one free" promotion. Sadly, nothing is truly free; the sale value covers all costs. This is one of the facts most ignored by consumers.

10. Expert technique and scientific evidence: This is the quintessential argument from authority in the modern world. This strategy relies on the apparent expertise of subject-matter experts. These strategies often include combined logical evidence such as charts, diagrams, statistics, and other visual aids.

Scientists, professors, physicians, and other experts are frequently included in advertising and commercials to provide credibility for the product or service. It often succeeds since many people believe in scientists and scientific data without question. However, it is critical to scrutinize the "proof" since it might be misleading.

11. Exaggeration: The use of hyperbole in advertising is often in the form of exaggeration. Exaggeration usually involves the use of "innocent superlatives". The primary objective of exaggeration is again to appeal to consumers' emotions rather than reason. Superlatives create far stronger imagery in the minds of consumers.

12. Humor: Humor is used in many commercials as an effective persuasive tool. Advertisers make people laugh to make them feel good about their products. It also works well as a disarming device because people tend to lower their guard when laughing. They aren't focused enough to observe details while enjoying a joke.

Humor is a very powerful device. Consider the use of humor in a magic act. Most successful magicians have some elements of humor in their shows because the humor aids their sleight of hand and other illusions by distracting the audience.

13. Explicit claims: If expressed or shown clearly, a claim is explicit. Some adverts, for example, list the major components, the price, the location of manufacturing, the quantity, efficacy, and dependability. Of course, such assertions should be demonstrated to be true or false, which is why few marketers make such explicit claims. If they turn out to be untrue, the advertiser may face issues. Thus, direct claims are rarely used, but when they are used, their rarity makes the ad more powerful.

14. Unfinished ads: These advertisements just toy with language by claiming their products work better than their rival's products without specifying how much better. This deliberate ploy looks to muddle consumers' minds while avoiding giving the consumer too much to think about.

15. Patriotic advertisements: These advertisements affirm that people support their country by using their products or service. This could work with any emotion in general. For example, in one advert, several brands banded together and announced that you would be helping a child go to school if you bought any of their products.

Another cellular phone company advertisement had a celebrity claiming that if people used this company's sim card, they would be helping to regulate the country's population! Evidently, even absurdity can be used in manipulative advertisements.

16. Questioning the customer: Advertisers who use this strategy provide questions to customers to get feedback on their products. This is the most direct method of doing market research. This is perhaps the most benign method because the customers have some choice in the matter.

Language manipulation may have a detrimental impact on customers, encouraging them to make illogical decisions. As advertising has become more sophisticated, objects are frequently presented as symbols of pleasure, love, and better lives rather than essential commodities.

Advertising should not instill in individuals the notion that materialism will bring them happiness or that declining to acquire useless items will make them miserable. Unfortunately, however, such ethical concerns do not disturb many companies.

Nevertheless, advertising is still vital since it is often the customer's primary source of information, and corporations should just be held accountable for providing accurate information. But they are not, as consumers do not have access to any serious systematic recourse. This is why so many examples of manipulative advertising and business practices are seen worldwide.

Examples of manipulative advertisements from real life

At this juncture, it would be beneficial to see some real-life examples of dark-psychological practices in advertising.

1. Let us look at the example of amusement parks. I have noticed the asphalt roads in all the amusement parks I have been to. In my teenage days, it used to irk me no end because, in the summer, the asphalt roads would lead to blistering heat.

Later I learned that this ploy was deliberate. Many of the shaded areas in amusement parks are filled with food stalls and other shops. It has even been suggested that amusement parks pump in food-related scents in areas close to food stalls. Smell is a powerful motivator of hunger, especially when combined with the asphalt-induced hellish heat and the shade provided by the covered food stall sections.

Add to this the common rule in many amusement parks whereby we are barred from bringing food from outside. Is it any wonder then that people spend far more money buying food and drinks than they spend to enter the park and use the rides? When the clearly higher food prices in such parks are taken into account, it is evident that amusement parks make a massive share of their profits from food and refreshment sales.

The manipulation there can even be so severe that one of the most famous amusement parks in the world will run their AC on full power in one particular shop during the middle of the summer. Sounds reasonable? Well, consider that this is the one shop selling sweatshirts and other cold-defeating items.

They know customers will feel guilty for enjoying the cold AC in the shop without buying anything. It is even possible the shopkeepers may ask a person to leave the "cold shop" if they do not buy something. Such overt cases of manipulation also exist.

2. The famous foot-in-the-door and reverse door-in-the-face techniques were explored in the Persuasion chapters. These techniques are extremely over-used in advertising and will not be discussed here to avoid repetition. Subliminal messaging is another supposedly effective tool that works on many people. Most of the claimed subliminal manipulation tools are allegedly sex-related and are used because sex sells. It is that simple.

3. An even more universally used method is the discount method: Make the original price quite outrageous and mark everything down twenty-seventy percent off, so the shoppers feel like they're getting a great deal. The unbelievable part about this is that millions of people fall for this trick every day.

4. Yet another case of manipulation can be witnessed in airports. It is interesting how stores are set up in US airports. Food stores will usually be on the left side of walkways (towards terminals, for example) because people walk on the right side. Builders know that hungry people will go to the food stores regardless of where it is. So, the clothing and other "luxuries" are on the right side, where we are more likely to stop and browse, and food is on the left because we'll go out of our way for it.

5. Some underhanded tactics are mundanely common in the cosmetics industry. Have you ever seen the slogan, "Because you can be even MORE perfect?" The beauty and fashion industries are masters at appearing to boost the ego while making the prey feel inadequate underneath.

6. Some furniture stores strategically place mirrors throughout the store to make you fall in love with their showrooms. According to this device, the "best item in the store is you," and people like looking at themselves. So if you see yourself in that new living room with a mirror and like what you see, you are more likely to buy it. Most showrooms are also built to be an ideal that people strive toward. Each showroom can have a whole backstory, including an ideal consumer who would live there.

Thus, when you see yourself in the mirror there, you see yourself in an ideal world, and being able to see yourself in that life is a step towards making it a reality. With that, you are now more likely to buy into and surround yourself with things from that lifestyle, meaning from that room. Many people who walk out of furniture shops with an undeniable sense of happiness have testified to this. The visual is that powerful.

7. A sign at a department store said: Spend Less, Get More, Be Happy. Nothing subtle about it, and yet it proved incredibly potent.

8. The knowledge about dark patterns could explain why we usually get better tickets or accommodation offers if we use Firefox on Windows than Safari and OSX. Dark pattern-based designs exploit Apple users' willingness to pay more for luxury items and services.

9. Yet another example is the practice of tokenism, commonly seen in advertising that uses the disabled community. Disabled people may be used in ads to make the viewers spend their money because they feel they are helping disabled people.

10. Have you ever noticed that some grocery stores prefer you enter on the right side of the store and then work your way counter-clockwise? This takes you past the donuts, and other sweets which hungry and impulse-buying customers will hopefully buy. In addition, lights are used in some supermarkets to make fruits and vegetables appear riper and healthier than they really are.

11. Another common practice in inventory stocking is how people stock more expensive products at eye-level on the shelves with lower-priced goods at the bottom. Moreover, they also put recently arrived perishable goods in the back with the older products in the front.

12. According to market research, when buying in-store, customers were more likely to purchase an item after holding it for more than thirty seconds. The percentage difference was over seventy-five percent.

13. Many Facebook campaigns say things like, "We're going out of business – 90% off!!!!" If you go to their page, you'll see that the page was created recently. The tactic works! They have to pay a few hundred dollars to have their ad seen by hundreds of thousands of people. Then they sell regular-priced items with high shipping costs.

14. Soft drinks in advertisements are laced with antacids to make them appear fizzy. That's what makes them so appealing. Antacids are hidden beneath all of those bubbles and tempting froth!

15. To keep vegetables and fruits looking fresh in ads, they sometimes use hair spray and deodorant. And you probably thought "freshness" came naturally. Sadly not! The vegetables and fruits look "fresh" because of glistening hair spray (and occasionally deodorant).

These were just some of the examples of manipulative advertisements. The entire list of manipulative practices utilized by devious entities is infinite. Ten chapters have been dedicated to showing how pervasive and varied manipulation is today.

This book about Dark Psychology has been quite dark till now. It is time to bring some powerful light into this. We now move into the climax chapter of this work: the real reason this book was written in the first place — to defend against this menace.

References:

Chandler, A. D. (1977). *The visible hand: The managerial revolution in American business.* Cambridge: Belknap Press.

Dale, J. P., Goggin, J., Leyda, J., McIntyre, A. P., & Negra, D. (Eds.). (2016). The aesthetics and affects of cuteness. Routledge.

Ellul, J. (1965). *Propaganda: The Formation of Men's Attitudes.* New York: Vintage Books, p. 64.

Hoffman, D. A. (2006). The Best Puffery Article Ever. *Iowa Law Review 91,* 1395.

https://datasociety.net/library/weaponizing-the-digital-influence-machine/

John, R. R. (2010). *Network nation: Inventing American telecommunications.* Cambridge: Belknap Press.

Moran, N. Illusion of safety: How consumers underestimate manipulation and deception in online (vs. offline) shopping contexts. J Consum Aff. 2020; 54: 890– 911

MSG Management Study Guide. Advertising Techniques - 13 Most Common Techniques Used by the Advertisers. (n.d.). Retrieved April 14, 2022, from https://www.managementstudyguide.com/advertising-techniques.htm

Niesen, M. (2015). From Gray Panther to National Nanny: the Kidvid Crusade and the Eclipse of the U.S. Federal Trade Commission, 1977–1980. *Communication, Culture & Critique* 8, 576–593.

Posted by Amanda Penn | Feb 1, & Penn, A. (2022, March 30). Manipulative advertising: 6 dirty tricks and examples. Shortform Books. Retrieved April 14, 2022, from https://www.shortform.com/blog/manipulative-advertising

Schudson, M. (1984). *Advertising, the Uneasy Persuasion: Its Dubious Impact on American Society.* New York: Basic Books.

Scott, S. (2017, November 21). What are the elements of false advertising? Small Business - Chron.com. Retrieved April 14, 2022, from https://smallbusiness.chron.com/elements-false-advertising-10139.html

Stole, I. (2000). Consumer protection in historical perspective: The five-year battle over Federal regulation of advertising, 1933–1958. *Mass Communication & Society 3*(4), 351–372.

Stole, I. (2000). Consumer protection in historical perspective: The five-year battle over Federal regulation of advertising, 1933–1958. *Mass Communication & Society 3*(4), 351–372, p. 367.

Key Chapter Ten Takeaways

1. Advertisements are mass persuasion campaigns designed to indirectly take money from consumers.

2. The three primary methods used in advertising include targeting Consumer Pain and Pleasure Points, Selling a Dream Outcome, and Reusing Successful Ad Concepts.

3. The methods used in psychologically manipulative advertising include: Association, Beautiful People, Warm and Fuzzy Feelings, Nostalgia Generation, Intensity and Weasel Words, Celebrity Endorsement, Plain Folk's Method, Flattery, Bribery, Expert "Evidence.", Exaggeration, Humor, Explicit Claims, Incomplete Ads, Patriotic Ads, Customer Questioning, etc.

PART IV

THE REAL DEFENSE AGAINST
THE DARK ARTS

CHAPTER ELEVEN
RESISTING MANIPULATION

And this is it! The Climax: the reason I wanted to write this book and why I had to include all those previous chapters. Defending against manipulation, fighting back against evil, helping people protect what is theirs, etc., are the drivers behind my making this book.

After studying the Dark Patterns subject during my work, I did an in-depth study of all the severe types of manipulation I could identify. It was only after that research that a serious, logical, and rational exploration of a defense could be ascertained.

This need is why the various types of manipulation have been examined in the previous chapters. Now that you know how to identify the different kinds of manipulation, how can you protect yourself from this?

While knowledge and awareness are the most crucial steps, there are some practices that you can employ to help prevent yourself from being manipulated by others. The goal of this chapter is to elucidate such tactics.

This chapter was created after long hours of analyzing the work of three Nobel laureates, a few world-renowned experts, some recent scholars, and considerable scientific research. All that work was used to synthesize a way to successfully defend against psychological manipulation, aka dark psychology.

The Noble Laureates whose work helped write this section include Ivan Pavlov, Richard Thaler, and Daniel Kahneman. So, behavioral economics is of obvious importance in this context. Also included in the creation of this chapter were the works of Noam Chomsky, Thomas Sowell, Daniel Goleman, and others. They noted the importance of linguistics, emotional intelligence, and political economics in presenting a viable defense against manipulation.

If one had to oversimplify the theme of this vital chapter and describe it in the briefest way possible, it would be the following. The key to defending against manipulation rests solely on one's ability to be an absolute intellectual tyrant to oneself while being focused on constant personal growth. Now let's explore this concept in more detail.

We will begin by understanding the term "Cognitive Load". In cognitive psychology, cognitive load refers to the quantity of working memory and information-processing capacity used during a particular task. Working memory is very limited in capability and the time it can be sustained. Working memory overload can severely impede learning. Distractions can worsen that overload.

Therefore, reducing cognitive load would be ideal for better intellectual functioning. A logical mindset is one of the best tools to combat manipulation. This allows one to become good at pattern recognition. Identifying patterns is a high-functioning skill and is indicative of a superior intellect.

At this point in your reading, I presume you have a solid knowledge of manipulation in terms of what it is, how it occurs, and the strategies involved. People who discover they have been duped may feel humiliated, weak, manipulated, or foolish.

Thus, we must be competent at noticing trends and patterns to avoid such defeats and failures. When someone manipulates us for their benefit, we become the losers in that scenario. They have defeated us. They have taken what is ours, be it time, money, or freedom. It is this victory-defeat theme that is incorporated into this entire chapter.

Let us now delve into why this manipulation-defeat recognition is valid and necessary. Some of us may be hesitant to recognize it as such, but reality does not depend on opinions. Being influenced can be irksome, especially after discovering that we have been exploited to assist someone further their selfish ambitions.

Constant manipulation can have disastrous consequences for the victims. The most obvious result is that the affected individual develops a negative attitude about themselves and the world. This is often true, especially for persons who have been deceived and mistreated.

Some people stop trusting anyone and everything for fear of being taken advantage of again. Nobody wants to lose their sense of self, self-respect, and pride. Most of all, they do not want to lose their precious and hard-earned resources.

Nonetheless, there is some fantastic news. Just as we can put measures in place to avoid illness, we can also put processes in place to prevent and avoid manipulation to a significant degree. Manipulation will usually only impact us if we let it or fail to recognize and stop it.

Unfortunately, some forms of manipulation are tough to resist because of factors out of individual control. Ergo, it is incumbent upon us to save every little bit of what is ours in the face of such powerful manipulation.

It is difficult to resist everyday deception from the media, family, friends, work, and relationships. Some people appear to learn nothing from prior manipulation since they continue to fall for it. This happens despite a willingness to stand up for themselves and a desire not to be exploited. There, then, is our first lesson: desire alone is irrelevant. We need the know-how. We need to recognize that it is going to be complicated.

Nevertheless, before you beat yourself up, remember that it's not only you that is struggling. Resisting manipulation is challenging for everyone, even if it may not appear so. Even the smartest individuals can be vulnerable to manipulation.

Suppose a logical mindset enables skillful pattern recognition, which supposedly helps counter manipulation. In that case, rationally, the opposite is true when it comes to falling victim to deception. The opposite of a logical mindset is an illogical one. The opposite of an objective mindset is a subjective one. And a subjective perspective often succumbs to overt emotionalism.

Based on everything explored so far, it is obvious that the primary weapon one needs to resist manipulation is the right personality. Hence, let us now learn about the personality profile that you need to program into yourself to defeat dark psychology: the Counter-mach.

The COUNTER-MACH

During the study of the Dark Triad, we examined Machiavellianism. The adjective, machiavellian implies something or someone who is cunning, scheming, and unscrupulous. There is an actual term for a person who has high machiavellianism. They are called High Machs.

When inventing the personality profile designed to counter manipulation, I decided to name it the Counter-Mach. As the name suggests, the idea is to counter machiavellian manipulation. In order to craft this Counter-Mach personality profile, I utilized the work of Nobel Prize winners, sport psychologists, business educators, etc. Consequently, there are two tools that are essential when it comes to successfully becoming a Counter-Mach.

1. Thinking correctly

In a hyper-emotional scenario, resistance is difficult. This is because we become closed-minded. Moreover, prior trauma, sometimes known as "baggage," can cause us to become emotional (either good or bad) in particular situations, and this emotionalism prevents us from perceiving ulterior motives clearly. Thinking correctly in a consistent fashion thus involves being logical.

The Counter-Mach relies on minimizing the use of mental shortcuts, prejudices, biases, etc., and resorts to keeping an open mind. Counter-Machs stay informed as much as possible and uses slow logical thinking to make prudent judgments everytime. They must avoid the traps of emotionalism and subjectivity.

Under emotionalism, we cannot see the broader picture or the hidden agendas at work simply because we are not in control of our faculties. This tells us what a logical mind gives us: control. Control gives Counter-Machs what we lack when we are manipulated: power!

Emotionalism and subjective thinking can be understood better through the concept of heuristics. In psychology, it is understood that people often use mental shortcuts when making decisions, which may not lead to perfect outcomes, but can produce optimal results. These are mental heuristics. This use of heuristics can lead to cognitive biases and irrational thinking, which are two undesirable outcomes for preventing manipulation. (*Kahneman & Charan, 2013*)

Some ways people can use to become high-caliber Counter-Machs include:-

- Forging a unique set of experiences and expertise.
- Paying close attention to ideas that are rejected by the popular majority. And while doing so, one should balance their open mind with intelligent skepticism.
- If one must have biases have postjudices, not prejudices. Examine facts before forming opinions. Also, realize that people don't have to be opinionated about everything because they cannot know everything.
- Always ask a lot of questions whenever you encounter something. Scientific inquiry is the foundation of the scientific method.

Often, the irrational emotionalism that renders people vulnerable, results in unwarranted fast thinking, which then ends with unfavorable outcomes. Human thinking can be divided into two types. Protocol One refers to the thinking people do, which is intuitive, emotional, and fast. Protocol Two is the kind of thinking which is inherently slower, more logical, and more controlled. Clearly, barring exceptional extreme situations, Protocol Two should be the basis for successful decision-making. (*Kahneman, 2011*)

The above Nobel prize-winning concept explains how and why manipulators try to make their targets emotional when manipulating them. People who are rendered incapable of making rational and logical decisions will rarely be able to defend themselves against manipulation. Counter-Machs buck this trend by also hiding their thoughts to stop manipulators from acquiring any knowledge about the Counter-Mach.

The effect of this can be experienced even in cases of mass manipulation. Ideally, the consumer is a "homo economicus," i.e., a person who behaves in accordance with their rational self-interest. If they are not, nudge systems may be implemented, using subtle manipulation to steer people into acting in a particular way. Nudge theory is also a potent behavioral economics theory that involves Nobel prize-winning research. (*Thaler & Sunstein, 2008*).

Thus, emotional irrationality can make people susceptible to individual and mass manipulation. It is therefore vital to be emotionally intelligent.

2. Emotional intelligence

Emotional intelligence, sometimes called emotional quotient (EQ), is the ability to correctly identify, comprehend, utilize, manage, and handle emotions. People with high EQ can read the emotions of others, but they can also recognize their own feelings and control them appropriately. It is this latter ability that is of particular significance in this context. (*Goleman, 1995*)

There are several tests out there that can test EI or emotional intelligence. The Mayer-Salovey-Caruso Emotional Intelligence Test is well known. Queendom.com also has an EI test. It is essential to do these tests because they tell us how capable we are, and more importantly, they tell us precisely what abilities lead to better EI.

There are traditionally five areas where competence indicates greater emotional intelligence. These include: Knowing one's emotions, managing relationships, Self-Motivation, Recognizing the feelings of others, and most tellingly, the ability to control one's emotional expressions. One proficiency that translates to reasonable competence in the above five areas is skilled self-awareness. (*Harvard Business Review, 2018*)

The Counter-Mach is emotionally adept and has a significant amount of emotional intelligence. They are typically more self-aware than the majority of the human population. Counter-Machs do a lot of personality and self-awareness tests to learn about themselves. They identify their weak areas and then begin to resolve them.

Correct thinking and emotional intelligence are the most valuable tools to resist manipulation. These tools can be considered as the input products that create a Counter-Mach. But what exactly does a Counter-Mach's personality look like? Counter-Machs defeat Dark Psychology by developing the following behavioral patterns.

Counter-Mach Behavior Patterns for Defeating Dark Psychology

1. Make your default state "NO".

It was arduous to choose which technique should be listed first. I find this behavioral choice to be the best option. Counter-Machs can even be recognized with this behavior. This tactic is based on the higher-order brain function of reprogramming ourselves and our behavior. This adaptability is a sign of human intelligence; fortunately, anyone can utilize this method.

One of the main reasons so many people succumb to malicious manipulation is that they react emotionally to external stimuli. This implies that the victims often resort to quick Protocol One thinking that is more automatic, intuitive, and illogical.

This practice is most noticeable in cases where someone requests something of you. Unfortunately, many people have this misconception of niceness instilled in them through social conditioning and nature. Hence, they often agree to the request automatically, without thinking it through. The reason for this behavior can be attributed to their being in a default "Yes" state. So, they must go out of their way to deny a request.

Since we need more time to think correctly, as Protocol Two indicates, the logical answer would be to make our default state "No," or, in other words, we must automatically deny every request made to us. Now, this does not mean that we directly reject the request outright.

No, Counter-Machs must not voice their denial but instead think about it. And then, they must try to convince themselves objectively why the request should be granted. In this case, they must consider the following questions:

- Is the person making the request important to them?
- Is the request valid?

- What does it cost them to accede to the request?
- What will they gain from fulfilling the request?

The correct answers to these questions will determine if they will succumb to potential manipulation. Remember, one has to only deny requests in their minds to provide them extra time to think. Counter-Machs do this to have enough time to analyze the situation logically. After the analysis, they could agree to the request. But then, the agreement would be because they decided that doing so would not be harmful to them.

By being programmed to respond negatively, one can also develop the exceptional ability to think things through even when there are distractions. This is called "Noise", which can significantly hinder our ability to think correctly. (*Kahneman et al., 2021*) Counter-Machs are competent at avoiding this "noise" because they are adept in focusing on what is important and tuning out the rest.

This method is not a foolproof strategy to avoid manipulation because it clearly depends on one's intelligence and wisdom. However, it will greatly limit the chances of people falling prey to psychological malice.

2. Maintain a journal

Earlier, we checked out the concept of cognitive load. A constant high level of cognitive load can cause a lot of stress. Fortunately, there is a great way to counter this problem and even make cognitive loading more efficient. First, maintain a digital journal of your daily life. In bygone days, people wrote diaries. That takes time. Today, technology is so advanced that writing a journal is easy, and there is no excuse for not utilizing this essential function.

Counter-Machs never rely on their memory alone and try to record everything of import. A digital journal allows you to use talk-to-text features and also allows you to track it more easily. In addition, it can be password-protected and stored safely both online and on your personal devices.

But why is this so important? Not relying on our memory to make prudent decisions is absolutely vital to making the right judgment call. Most cognitive biases are a result of emotionalism and prior experiences. In order to think correctly, we need facts and data. Think about the usefulness of having a journal when it comes to gaslighting.

If someone is lying or deceiving you in any way or trying to distort reality, being able to refer back to the day in question could be very beneficial. In fact, checking what happened could prove instrumental in defeating the manipulation. Thus, you should develop the habit of creating a daily journal where you note down the most noteworthy events of the day.

Another tactic would be to note the unexpected emotions you felt on the day. Apart from recording what happened, recording your reaction to it could be a convenient tool. Save the last 20-30 minutes before sleep to record the daily details in your journal/diary.

3. Know yourself fully but do not give others that privilege

Privacy is the most defining feature of liberty. True freedom does not exist if you do not have real privacy. When we talk about privacy, we are talking about privacy in your private space, which is your own space. Counter-Machs have to be masters of privacy and skilled at protecting it.

Privacy is a right, but it is also incumbent upon us to not foolishly destroy our own privacy because of weaknesses. By now, it ought to be clear that knowledge is the greatest asset to solving any problem. Similarly, knowledge of their victims is crucial to success for a manipulator. Hence, a victim would be anything but wise if they provide the knowledge themselves.

The main culprit in this regard is the utter weakness some people have for affirmations from others. This is, of course, seen in attention-seeking behavior on social media. Posting your pictures, thoughts, etc., in a vain attempt to find positive attention from others, including strangers, is a colossal weakness that inhibits accurate thinking and self-mastery.

Any person who needs affirmation from others to feel good about themselves has lost already because they have given control and power over their lives to the whims of others. Successfully combating manipulation requires us to keep as much information as possible about us secret and private. In this digital surveillance age, it is already incredibly difficult to do so. Thus, people destroying their own privacy is all the more shocking.

4. Choose the correct axioms for your life

An axiom is a self-evident truth. This means that you do not need to prove it. Axioms are used in mathematics too, but in the case of human behavior and psychology, it refers to one's fundamental principles. These rules are part of your moral core and the principles you must never compromise on. Personal axioms are often the main reason for a person's behavior.

Life>Liberty>Pursuit of Happiness is an excellent axiomatic motto to live by and it is the foundational moral core driving Counter-Machs. Notice the sign used between the three concepts. This clearly reveals which is more important than the other. Now you must use this when analyzing things for decision-making. For example, suppose something is detrimental to your life, liberty, or pursuit of happiness. In that case, it should be considered bad; therefore, you must discard it.

The trick is using this correctly when something fulfills one or two of the three but not all of them. That is when the ">" symbol comes in handy. If something is good for pursuing happiness and liberty but bad for your life, it should be discarded. Drug use is an excellent example of such a concept, as is smoking and alcohol drinking.

This axiomatic foundation can help you distinguish between good and bad choices and thus help you avoid manipulation.

5. Stay aware and keep your distance

A manipulator may be identified by observing how a person behaves with different individuals and in various situations. While we all have had some degree of social differentiation, certain psychological manipulators have a history of existing in extremes, being extremely courteous to one person and cruel to another or pathetically helpless one minute and ferociously aggressive the next.

When you see someone behaving this way frequently, keep a safe distance and avoid dealing with them unless absolutely necessary. As previously stated, the causes of persistent psychological manipulation are multifaceted and deep-seated. It is not your responsibility to alter psychopaths.

Thus, history is of paramount importance. Everything in the present happens because of past actions. A person with a history of bad behavior deserves to be judged for it. One of the most accursed practices that lead to people suffering from manipulation is the foolish notion, "Do not judge." We must learn to judge correctly. The right path to success and victory is laden with decisions based on judgments. Counter-Machs are strong judges who never shirk from utilizing prudent judgments because of emotionalism.

6. Set boundaries and enforce consequences

When a manipulator persists in crossing your limits and refuses to accept "no" for an answer, inform them of the negative consequences of their behavior. Utilize your ability to define negative effect (s) to force a problematic individual to stand down.

Knowing about the consequences may make the manipulative person pause. As a result, self-respect, which was damaged by the manipulator's wrongdoing, can be restored. This ability and the fortitude to see it to its conclusion can have a lifesaving impact.

Now, let us go into more specific details that will allow Counter-Machs to deal with particular kinds of manipulation. Apart from these broad internal techniques based on thinking, you can also incorporate linguistic-based behavioral patterns to deal with manipulation attempts.

Part 1: Defending against individual manipulation

We shall first look at potent defense mechanisms to counter manipulation at an interpersonal level. This is about adopting proven behaviors to disrupt dark psychological attempts. They require practice and dedication on your part. Study them thoroughly and become a potent Counter-Mach. It is recommended to try to practice them in front of a mirror, so it becomes a habit.

Manipulation-negating behavioral techniques

When manipulators deny or try to confuse what you are saying, the following behaviors can be helpful for you to employ.

1. Broken record approach

Choose a short statement or sentence and repeat it, such as, "The chocolate is gone", "I'm not buying anything today," or "I demand a refund for this faulty item." While you may briefly recognize hearing what another person says, such as "Yes, I understand, and as I was saying" or "Yes, I understand, and I still want" or "Yes, and going back to the topic," you must remain on-point, on-task, and on-message.

This minimizes the chances that you will be swayed by the other person's rhetoric and demands. It does this by preserving your focus on what you are saying. It also helps to prevent getting distracted. Avoiding "Noise" is critical to being able to exercise prudent judgment. (*Kahneman et al., 2021*)

2. Content-to-process

You intelligently change your focus from the issue or content of the discussion, to the form or method of the interaction. Examples of this will sound similar to, "Wow, you seem to be becoming really angry with me", "Now we're getting involved in unnecessary matters," or "I see that you keep shifting the topic rather than staying on the topic I'm bringing up and would like to really discuss."

This behavior can disrupt the manipulator because it tells them that you have noticed their method of discourse and are thus an intelligent person. You will immediately appear more potent; therefore, preying on you would seem very risky. This might be more than enough for them to stop trying to manipulate you.

3. Defusing

Given the other person's rage or emotional reaction, you pause the conversation until he has cooled down and can carry on a constructive discourse. You can use comments such as, "Let's stop now and resume once you've calmed down", or "I realize how tremendously tough and emotionally unpleasant this conversation is for you, so let's speak more tomorrow."

This is a clear use of superior emotional intelligence and slow thinking. Keeping the conversation under your control reduces the chances of succumbing to emotional outbursts and faulty thinking. It is equivalent to defusing the enemy's weapons and stopping them from damaging you.

4. Assertive delay

You purposefully postpone replying to a hard message until you are relaxed and ready to handle it effectively. For example, you may say, "I'll think about this and get back to you," or "I want to reserve judgment for now, and I will handle this later."

This behavior is akin to the practice mentioned earlier of making your default state "No." By constantly refusing to respond immediately, you are using your slow, logical thinking system to make sure that you do not easily succumb to the devious machinations of another.

5. Assertive inquiry

Challenge the criticism to find out what's really behind it. For example, "Since your outrage appears to be out of proportion to the circumstances, what are you really upset about?", "Did something happen that I'm not aware of?", "I wonder what bothers you so much about my speaking out?", or "What appears to be your issue with my comments?".

Such questions exude so much unconscious power that they can disrupt even the suavest manipulators. This tactic has the double effect of simultaneously showing the manipulator how immune you are and how dangerous an opponent you can be.

6. Assertive agreement

Accept, acknowledge, and sometimes even express gratitude for any specific complaint or critical feedback you can agree with. For example, "I did not do my best in handling that situation," or "I was late for that meeting," etc.

Such admissions indicate that you are a person who is most comfortable admitting your own shortcomings. As a result, you instantly appear competent in exercising self-control and have a lot of self-assurance. Yet again, this is a sign of superior emotional intelligence, which is one principal guarantor of immunity against manipulation.

Using genuine agreement in such a surgical manner may give you great defensive ability against manipulation. Moreover, agreeing with the manipulator may also throw them off their game. Assertive agreement is a risky tactic that should be carefully and sparingly used.

7. Clouding

Refuse to address any complaint, criticism, or put down, and instead only address complaints or critical remarks with which you agree. You can do this by rephrasing the criticism as something you can honestly agree with. You need to be well-versed in rhetoric to pull this off. Linguistic skill is an invaluable tool when it comes to resisting manipulation.

This method is similar to the "strawman" argumentation fallacy. It is an advanced tactic that is almost like manipulating the manipulator because it helps you turn the tables on the person trying to coerce you.

Clouding is similar to emotional masking in principle. You twist the manipulator's words and refuse to conform to their actual message. You will protect yourself quite well if you can use this clouding technique correctly.

Apart from these seven general defensive techniques, here is a list of tactical sentences specially designed to counter gaslighting.

Fighting Gaslighting

The following list of 20 statements is designed to counter the most common gaslighting claims used by manipulators. 1-4 are responses to tackle claims such as "You are overreacting". 5-8 includes answers that can help with gaslighting comments such as "You are too sensitive". 9-13 is about responding to ideas like

"You are imagining things". 14-16 is meant to check the lies gaslighters say when in denial, such as "I never said that". Lastly, 17-20 is to counter things like "It's not a big deal". (*Rana, 2022*)

1. "I am not overreacting; I am correctly dealing with the circumstances as I ought to be."

2. "You can disagree with my convictions, but that doesn't make my beliefs any less genuine or untrue."

3. "I do not have to persuade you of my feelings or their veracity; that's something you have to figure out for yourself."

4. "I will definitely not doubt myself because of your assertion. I know exactly what I feel and what I think, and I am going to follow my instincts."

5. "I am quite normal and am certainly not too sensitive."

6. "Being sensitive is not wrong, nor is it a problem."

7. "I will not apologize for having sentiments or being human."

8. "I have the right to feel anything I choose."

9. "I am aware of what I witnessed/heard, and I expect you to give me the truth."

10. "I'm not making it up; I'm simply seeing/hearing what's there."

11. "Why are you attempting to dupe me?"

12. "I'm not paranoid; I'm just paying attention."

13. "I'm not insane; I'm just seeing/hearing what's going on."

14. "I know what I heard/saw, and I won't doubt my memories."

15. "You may not recall saying or doing that, but I do, and it harmed me."

16. "I'm not sure why you're denying it, but I know what happened, and I'm not going to let you fool/gaslight me."

17. "This is really important to me, and I need you to respect my feelings."

18. "I understand you may not think it's a big thing, but it is to me, and I need your help."

19. "Just because you don't believe my feelings are valid doesn't mean they aren't real."

20. "I'm not going to overlook my mental health because you don't believe it's important." (*Rana, 2022*)

Countering manipulators' response to anti-manipulation

Do not presume that the aforementioned seven behavioral techniques will automatically end all manipulation attempts. Manipulators may try to oppose these tactics. Counter-Machs have to be adept at overcoming the manipulator's defensive attempts. We can look at some of the more common behaviors manipulators exhibit to try and counter your defenses and what you can do to counteract them.

1. Laughing it off

Here, the manipulator will try to laugh at your anti-manipulation behavior. You can then use the Broken Record or the Content-to-Process Shift technique to disrupt the enemy further. But what you must never do is to "take insult" at their insulting, outrageous behavior. This emotional reaction is what the manipulator is aiming at when using the "Laughing-it-off" technique. (*Friedman, 2022*)

Once again, emotional intelligence is required to challenge and defeat those trying to manipulate you.

2. Accusing gambit

You are blatantly blamed for some problem. You can calmly disagree or use Assertive Inquiry. If the manipulator persists, you may try to continue with Clouding or a cautious Assertive Agreement. (*Friedman, 2022*) This method makes the manipulator think they have won, but you manipulate them instead.

3. The beat-up

Your defense can be met with a personal attack and character assassination. The Broken Record or Defusing techniques could work here, but "Assertive Irony" ("Thanks") may be a good technique in this case. It is hard to pull off, but sarcasm can irritate people, and manipulators do not deserve mercy from their intended victims. (*Friedman, 2022*) When an enemy wants to harm you, do not hesitate to use sarcasm as a weapon.

4. Delaying gambit

The other person wishes to postpone their response because they are tired or simply dismiss it as inconvenient. You can use the Broken Record technique or merely insist on a specific time and date when the issue can be thoroughly examined and resolved. (*Friedman, 2022*)

5. "Why" gambit

All your assertions are repeatedly thwarted by the manipulator asking, "Why?". Aside from using the Broken Record once more, you could use a targeted Content-to-Process Shift such as "It's not about 'why' anything. That's not the point. The real problem is...". Such questions are designed to unsettle the manipulator by forcing them to stop and think. This can break their flow, and since you are not answering their "Why" query, they will cease. (*Friedman, 2022*)

6. Self-pity gambit

Your defense is met with sadness, tears, and turning away. This is a vain attempt to convey that by continuing this conversational thread, you are being hurtfully sadistic. You must use Assertive Agreement (e.g., "I understand this is a complex topic, and we must resolve it.") and deny any such attempts to evoke your pity. (*Friedman, 2022*) Any such maneuver can destroy your entire defense.

7. Quibbling

The person will try to pettily argue about the legitimacy of your feelings or thoughts, the severity of the problem, or whether they want to address it at all. Use a technique such Content-to-Process Shift, Defusing, or Assertive Delay to counter their malice. (*Friedman, 2022*)

8. Threats

Your claim is met with a veiled indirect or overtly direct threat of negative consequences. Assertive Inquiry, Defusing, Assertive Delay, or Content-to-Process Shift are all options to counter this, but extra caution should be exercised. This is usually the toughest stratagem for innocent people to counter. We are not inherently malicious, and some may find it hard to deal with threats appropriately. (*Friedman, 2022*)

Unfortunately, you cannot indulge in such niceness. A threat may be a benign attempt to make you emotional and thus render you incompetent. Nevertheless, you cannot ignore it. Thinking correctly and maintaining high emotional intelligence are vital to preserving your life and liberty.

9. Denial

Your claim may be met with outright denials, such as "I didn't do that," "You misunderstood me," etc. Such denials may appear infantile and ridiculous, but they can prove very damning if they break through someone's defenses. This usually happens due to someone's "niceness", pity, or sympathy. (*Friedman, 2022*)

Analyzing people using dark psychology

One of the benefits of becoming aware of dark psychology is that you can use it against manipulators. Many books about dark psychology propose that body language analysis is an excellent method to analyze people. However, this idea is not correct. Body language is highly dependent on culture and ethnicity. It can vary depending on a person's personality too. An extrovert and an introvert will have markedly different body language responses to the same stimuli. Thus, true Counter-Machs will never resort to assessing body-language because it is futile in most environments.

This is attested to by the fact that body language is not sign language. Body language has no grammatical structure and remains ambiguous. Hence, while proxemics, opulesics, and haptics are valid fields of body language study involving physical proximity, eye movement, and touching, respectively, it is beyond the scope of this book because it does not provide a real benefit to learning or countering dark psychology.

Additionally, a former FBI officer, Joe Navarro, who has written some great books on body language, has also testified to the inaccuracy of most body language analysis techniques in the mainstream popular consciousness.

Apart from the sheer non-uniform nature of body language, another reason is that law enforcement studies the body language of people in a very controlled setting. A suspect will not act the same way in his comfortable home as he will act if he is being interrogated in a closed room at the police station. It is common sense.

When interrogating a person, it is usually done in a closed, controlled environment where the interrogator has an evident power and location advantage. The person being questioned is usually intimidated and experiencing stress which is where body language can be manipulated and studied enough to gain insights.

Nevertheless, it is possible to use dark psychology science to analyze people. Instead of body language, we can study personality traits and behavior. Personality is not superficial like body language. Studying personality allows for deeper insight into an individual's psyche, giving Counter-Machs more precise information about the kind of person someone is. This will allow us to make a more prudent judgment regarding potential manipulators.

The Dirty Dozen and the much more famous Psychopathy Checklist are excellent tools to help Counter-Machs analyze people's behavior.

Psychopaths, as explained before, are people who prey on others ruthlessly, using charm, deception, violence, or other methods to get what they want. Lack of a conscience or absence of a sense of guilt, lack of empathy, egocentricity, pathological lying, repeated violations of social norms, disregard for the law, shallow emotions, and a history of victimizing others, etc., are all potential symptoms of psychopathy.

Dark psychology checklist

When you meet people, it is good to analyze their behavior based on the following checklist. (*Hare, 1999*) It may not be immediately possible to gauge the answers for all the features, but the time required should not deter you. On the contrary, it could prove vital to your well-being. Nobody wants to waste their valuable time and life dealing with malicious people, do they?

Avoid people if they display many of the traits below and focus more on characteristics with the symbol ~ because they are more important indicators of malevolence.

- They are glib and display superficial charm.
- They need constant stimulation and can get bored quickly.
- They are pathological liars. ~
- They are cunning and manipulative. ~
- They show an unmistakable lack of remorse or guilt. ~
- They have a shallow affect (superficial emotional responsiveness) and sometimes show uncharacteristically overt emotionalism. (Dark Empath Alert!) ~
- They are often callous and immoral. This is a vital sign. ~
- They have a parasitic lifestyle. ~
- They have poor behavioral controls.
- They are sexually promiscuous. ~
- They have a history of early behavioral problems.
- They lack realistic long-term goals.
- They are impulsive.

- They are irresponsible. ~
- They often fail to accept responsibility for their own actions. ~
- They have many short-term marital and premarital relationships. ~
- They have had periods of juvenile delinquency. (*Hare, 1999*)

It may seem impractical to test everybody you meet using this checklist, but it is not as hard as it seems. Moreover, the difficulty does not diminish its immense value. As a Counter-Mach, you can make this task easier by checking the suspect's opinions on issues. Here are some examples of issues you can discuss with them to check their penchant for indulging in manipulative dark psychology.

Dark psychology inquiry topics

When interviewing people on the following topics, it is best to resort to more subtle and morally gray areas because they will be less likely to alert the manipulator to your true purpose. Here, we will take inspiration from conman Victor Lustig and his list, which we explored before.

- Question them about broad topics like socialism, communism, etc. If they indicate support for such anti-freedom ideas, mentally flag them for immorality. But overtly, accept their opinions with a smile and maybe even feign agreement.
- Check if they support high taxes and the obstruction of property ownership.
- Check if they support societal financial support of individuals' lifestyles and choices.
- Check if they support adultery, no-fault divorces, polyamory, and marital split of money during a divorce.
- Enquire if they support riotous protests, theft, property damage, etc.

These are generic issues and can seem innocent. However, a person's political views are the best means to gauge their true nature. In fact, it can prove instrumental to Counter-Machs when you are choosing a romantic partner or even benefit you in the workplace.

People who are anti-life, anti-liberty, and anti-individual are most likely to use dark psychology and manipulate people. The reasoning is simple. A manipulator is immoral, which is why they do not mind violating the freedoms of another. This will be reflected in their political views as well.

Part 2: Defending against mass manipulation

In Part 1 of this chapter, we looked at how best to defend against individual manipulation. Of course, that is vital, but it is also imperative to know how to protect against mass manipulation because it is way more evil and dangerous. If one manipulator can cause so much damage to someone, imagine what an entire system of nefariousness can do when heinous people use it. Counter-Machs must acquire protection against mass manipulation.

Remember that every system is only as good as the people running it. The danger is more severe in a system with an enormous power imbalance, such as between corporations and consumers or governments and citizens.

Let us look at the information medium first. Media manipulation is one of the biggest problems in the mass manipulation process. Hence, we must look to become informed citizens by developing a counter against media manipulation.

Persevering against media manipulation in the News.

News media is the most significant component of the mass media industry. It is also the most important one to consider when devising a method to counter media manipulation. When one goes into Google News for the first time, the headlines and news articles on the first page are very telling. They use geolocation to present news of events from your physical location.

However, it has been found that they also show news from only a select group of news sources. For example, in the World section of Google News, the most common news organizations are the New York Times, the Washington Post, Vox, CNN, HuffPost, Vanity Fair, Al-Jazeera, CBS, CTV, etc. That was surprising, to say the least.

The immensely valuable AllSides organization has clearly identified all the above-mentioned news organizations as leftist companies. A leftist organization, by definition, is inclined to be against freedom and is prone to manipulation, as was explored earlier. If the New York Times and the Washington Post appear suspect, one could always opt for the New York Post and the Washington Times.

Hence, we used AllSides to develop a list of neutral, unbiased, and anti-left news organizations.

Here is a list of such news organizations: The Associated Press, Reuters, the New York Post, the Washington Times, the Epoch Times, the Daily Wire, the Washington Examiner, The Hill, the Wall Street Journal, The Federalist, etc.

Once this list is made, go to the Google News page and, in the search bar, type the names of these news organizations separately. You will be taken to news from that source when you click Search. There you will also find the option to "FOLLOW" those news sources. Click on that, and then you will receive news from those sources over the other ones.

Do this with the news organizations of your country by finding out which of them are unbiased and genuine.

This is a much-needed step as the anti-liberty bias of all the left-leaning news organizations (as per AllSides) was checked and verified against the news about the same event in other unbiased, non-leftist, proper news sources. This is the best way to counter media manipulation.

You can curate the news content you are exposed to. Stop being manipulated by news media. Remember the agenda-setting theory function of the media, which was exposed and explored in a previous chapter. If one is short of time and cannot check the integrity of every news article, this method is the best way to counter media manipulation. Use Google News to remove the power of news media to manipulate you.

Conquering advertising manipulation

The primary tool to counter manipulative advertising is to use the default "No" response state. There is a reason why skepticism is often seen in more intelligent people. Do not accept anything and everything you are exposed to. Finally, and most importantly, NEVER make decisions based on emotions. Always be objective and logical. Be wary of your emotional response and remember the following.

1. Emotional ads try to manipulate consumers into making a purchasing decision based on desire rather than logic. Emotions and emotional thinking can never lead to favorable outcomes.

2. Identify whether your motivation to buy something is intrinsic or extrinsic. Always allow for a minute or two before making a final buying decision. During that minute, try to come up with as many reasons as possible for why you must buy something. A default negative disposition can thus help you to save your money.

3. Watch out for products indirectly targeted at you. Do as much research as possible before buying anything. Do you really need to buy something?

4. Ask yourself why you are reacting in a particular way. Was there an ad that triggered this response in you? This is often the best and easiest way to counter advertising manipulation of all sorts. This is self-realization. Make deliberate notes of all emotional changes within yourself. If you suddenly experience a difference in feeling, that should trigger immediate introspection and investigation.

Self-Awareness is your biggest ally against manipulation because it enables "Slow Thinking/ Protocol Two," also known as Logical thinking. It is like watching yourself do something. This detachment and distancing are what allow you to avoid committing grievous blunders.

Finally, always remember one essential rule. No advertisement has ever been made where the target consumer was the primary beneficiary. Advertisements are always for the benefit of the seller/producer— Always!

Protecting yourself against internet manipulation

Lastly, let us look at how we can defend ourselves against the most hazardous manipulation medium of the modern world. The internet is, without a doubt, one of the greatest inventions of humankind. The potential for human progress due to the internet is immense. Unfortunately, the internet is also the perfect tool for mass manipulation.

We have already explored how social media, news media, Big Tech, and others could inhibit liberty and quality-of-life, and cause emotional distress, financial mishaps, distortions of reality, etc. Yet, don't let the existence of such malice absolve you from your responsibility to protect and better yourself.

One of the cognitive skills Counter-Machs can use to change their behavior and decision-making is self-nudging. Self-nudging enables people to configure their digital environments to best suit them.

This may entail turning off app alerts or reorganizing one's smartphone home screen to show only relevant applications, such as the calendar, camera, navigation, and weather applications. In addition, things that are considered very distracting, such as gaming or social media, should be stored in folders. The researchers also advise users to set time limitations for their social media use.

The digital world is full of traps. Even so, you can take precautions to prevent falling into them. For example, you may turn off notifications from applications that constantly demand your attention in the same way that we would conceal your chocolate stockpile in the back of the closet and place a bowl of fruit on the table. This is the opposite of what Dark Patterns do. Here you are using visual cues to benefit you, unlike how dark patterns harm you.

And, just as we would glance right and left before crossing the street, we should make it a practice to ask specific questions to evaluate the material we see online. Questions such as where did the knowledge come from? Which sources were mentioned? Is it possible to discover comparable material on credible websites? Skepticism is once again our ally. Objective inquiry through the scientific method is the fundamental driver of human progress.

Now let us look at some essential practices to reduce our vulnerability to internet manipulation.

- Protect your digital devices with the appropriate anti-malware software. This includes firewalls, antivirus software, etc. In addition, run regular virus and malware scans on your computer.
- Use a VPN. Search online for the VPN service that is the most suitable one for you. ExpressVPN and NordVPN seem to be the most popular ones out there.
- Whenever you use your internet browser, it is recommended that you delete your cookies and your temporary internet files. It is also prudent to delete your browsing history when you are done.
- It is best not to put your pictures online on social media. Especially since, in this day and age, people are "canceled" for trivial things they said years ago. Thus one cannot afford to be lax about one's digital footprint.
- Furthermore, one should maintain more than one email address across multiple email providers. Gmail, Yahoomail, Hotmail, etc., are some of the better-known email service providers.
- Your phone can be used as a spying tool where tech companies and their algorithms track what you say to be able to use targeted advertising. Once you are finished with an online app on your phone, always make sure that you actually stop and close the app to ensure that it doesn't run in the background. The open app is how the bulk of the tracking is done. I have tested this out by having fake conversations about products and services in the presence of my phone. Sometime later, when I was on my laptop, I saw ads about the products I talked about on my social media, proving that manipulation and spying exist and that mobile phones are a tool through which such manipulation happens.

Big Data is also a great enabler of manipulation. For example, there are companies out there who indulge in mass data brokering. They steal consumer data without the customer's consent and sell it to whoever wants it. In 2019, the worldwide data-brokerage market amounted to around 230 billion dollars! And the data they collect includes the most personal data like race, sex, marital status, interests, location, etc.

- Hence, a paid service like DeleteMe could be a good tool for erasing your digital presence. You can even try doing it yourself using their link, https://joindeleteme.com/help/diy-free-opt-out-guide/

We have come to the end of this most important chapter. I recommend you print out this chapter and re-read it regularly until you have learned it thoroughly. This chapter began with a call to be a tyrant to yourself. This was a reference to the discipline and determination that would make you a Counter-Mach.

Do not ever compromise on the strategies and methods mentioned in this chapter. There will be no key takeaway section for this chapter. It is a deliberate choice. The entire chapter is written as briefly as possible, and it is so essential that the whole chapter is a takeaway by itself.

References:

"The Universal Declaration of Human Rights" (UDHR). United Nations General Assembly (1948)

Acquisti, A. (2009). Nudging privacy: The behavioral economics of personal information. IEEE security & privacy, 7(6), 82-85.

Acquisti, A., Adjerid, I., & Brandimarte, L. (2013). Gone in 15 seconds: The limits of privacy transparency and control. IEEE Security & Privacy, 11(4), 72-74.

Acquisti, A., John, L. K., & Loewenstein, G. (2013). What is privacy worth?. The Journal of Legal Studies, 42(2), 249-274.

Aglietta, M.; Reberioux, A.; Babiak, P. "Psychopathic Manipulation at Work", in Gacono, C.B. (Ed), The Clinical and Forensic Assessment of Psychopathy: A Practitioner's Guide, Erlbaum, Mahwah, NJ. (2000)

Babiak, P., & Hare, R. D. (2007). Snakes in Suits. Collins. https://doi.org/10.1604/9780061147890

Barrett, L., & Campbel, A. J. (2018). Request to Investigate Google's Unfair and Deceptive Practices in Marketing Apps for Children.

Bursten, Ben. "The Manipulative Personality". Archives of General Psychiatry, Vol 26 No 4. (1972)

Buss DM, Gomes M, Higgins DS, Lauterback K. "Tactics of Manipulation". Journal of Personality and Social Psychology, Vol 52 No 6 (1987)

Carr-Ruffino, Norma. "The Promotable Woman". Career Pr Inc; 4 ed. (2004)

DeGiulio A., Lee H., Birrell E. (2021) "Ask App Not to Track": The Effect of Opt-In Tracking Authorization on Mobile Privacy. In: Saracino A., Mori P. (eds) Emerging Technologies for Authorization and Authentication. ETAA 2021. Lecture Notes in Computer Science, vol 13136. Springer, Cham.

Friedman, B., & Hendry, D. G. (2019). Value sensitive design: Shaping technology with moral imagination. MIT Press.

Friedman, W. J. (n.d.). Developing An Inner Meter on Manipulation — A Critical Life Skill. Developing An Inner Meter on Manipulation — A Critical Life Skill - Wellness, Disease Prevention, And Stress

Reduction Information; www.mentalhelp.net. Retrieved May 15, 2022, from https://www.mentalhelp.net/blogs/developing-an-inner-meter-on-manipulation-a-critical-life-skill/

Goldsmith, R.E.; Freyd, J. (2005). "Effects of Emotional Abuse in Family and Work Environments". Journal of Emotional Abuse 5 (2005)

Goleman, D. (1995). Emotional Intelligence: Why It Can Matter More Than IQ. Bantam. https://doi.org/10.1604/9780553383713

Hare, R. D. (1999). Without Conscience. https://doi.org/10.1604/9781572304512

Kahneman, D. (2011). Thinking, Fast and Slow. Farrar, Straus and Giroux.

Kahneman, D., & Charan, R. (2013). HBR's 10 Must Reads on Making Smart Decisions. Harvard Business Review.

Kahneman, D., Sibony, O., & Sunstein, C. R. (2021). Noise: A Flaw in Human Judgment. Little, Brown and Company- Hachette Book Group.

Mason, P. T. & Kreger, R. (2010). Stop walking on eggshells: taking your life back when someone you care about has borderline personality disorder (second edition). New Harbinger Publications, Oakland, CA.

Moore, Thomas Geoffrey; Marie-France Hirigoyen; Helen Marx. "Stalking the Soul: Emotional Abuse and the Erosion of Identity". New York: Turtle Point Press. (2004)

Murdock, R. (2012, March 30). Retrieved from https://www.earlytorise.com/how-to-deal-with-manipulative-people–part-two/

Ni, P. (2014, June 1). How to spot and stop manipulators. Retrieved from https://www.psychologytoday.com/us/blog/communication-success/201406/ho…

Rana, D. (2022, April 27). 5 Gaslighting Phrases People Casually Use To Manipulate You | by Darshak Rana | Apr, 2022 | Better Humans. Medium; betterhumans.pub. https://betterhumans.pub/5-gaslighting-phrases-people-casually-use-to-manipulate-you-30da5c62048b

Review, H. B., Goleman, D., Kaplan, R. S., David, S., & Eurich, T. (2018). Self-Awareness (HBR Emotional Intelligence Series). Harvard Business Review.

Thaler, R. H., & Sunstein, C. R. (2008). Nudge: Improving Decisions about Health, Wealth, and Happiness. Yale University Press. https://doi.org/10.1604/9780300122237

Vakkuri, V., Kemell, K. K., & Abrahamsson, P. (2020, August). ECCOLA-a method for implementing ethically aligned AI systems. In 2020 46th Euromicro Conference on Software Engineering and Advanced Applications (SEAA) (pp. 195-204). IEEE.

Wijesekera, P., et al.: The feasibility of dynamically granted permissions: Aligning mobile privacy with user preferences. In: 2017 IEEE Symposium on Security and Privacy (SP), pp. 1077–1093.

FINAL WORDS

We've covered a wide range of issues in this book on manipulation, including what it is, what it could look like, and how to avoid it. We explored both individual manipulation and mass manipulation. In addition, we studied the signs and science behind dark psychology. You also know how to become a Counter-Mach.

We now need to recognize the historical roots of this problem. Humans have been manipulating one another since the beginning of time. People have been utilizing techniques to play on natural human emotions to gain what they want from others.

People have reached a certain level of power by promising false things or preying on primal human desires and people's anxieties. This has been accomplished by using immoral psychological tactics for the benefit of the predator and to the detriment of their victims. So while we now know more about mind games, we mustn't make the error of assuming that the principles behind them are anything new.

I hope this book has been educational and enlightening for you. I have endeavored to provide you with the most relevant information about dark psychology and manipulation available today.

Dark Psychology is a subject with surprisingly little information available online. Much of the available information seemed underwhelming, pseudo-scientific, and in some cases, downright false. That is why I was compelled to write this book.

But now, it is up to you to put your knowledge from this book into practice. You should now have the most up-to-date knowledge about manipulation and dark psychological trends.

This book provides everything to you in the simplest yet most effective language. Manipulation, particularly media manipulation, is contentious, with most people refusing to recognize it. Nevertheless, it is genuine. The scientific evidence provided, the practical, real-life instances shown, and the logical reasoning exercised on the subject are keener than the intellectual information available on many other issues.

After reading this book, nobody should ever fall into such evil individuals' clutches. The topics were explained in-depth, and examples were supplied at each stage to ensure that you can use the knowledge in real-life situations.

The essential parts of the book explored tried-and-tested ways of defending yourself against manipulation and detecting media manipulation. Hopefully, they will enable you to become a Counter-Mach and then you can protect your mind and general quality of life.

Additionally, a strong community of like-minded people is of paramount importance. It is more useful in collecting invaluable information which can be shared among each other. I have created a Facebook Group for you to join. Here you will get to meet similar people and obtain helpful information. You will also get first access to all subsequent books I publish. You can join the link at

https://www.facebook.com/groups/5031284973618613

As a bonus, I have also decided to provide another tool to help you optimize your life and further safeguard you from regressive problems like manipulation. Therefore, I have made a mini-ebook titled "Treasure of 100 Billions," which provides a life optimization plan, a life lessons list, and several affirmations geared to enhance personal growth.

A hundred billion indicates the total number of human beings thought to have ever existed in this world. In the mini ebook, I have compiled modern scientific breakthrough ideas and life lessons from ancient philosophical works that have stood the test of time. I have used wisdom from cultures as diverse as Greek, Roman, Chinese, Indian, Japanese, etc. You can obtain this ebook for free by scanning the QR code below.

You could also get it by going to:

https://phronesispublications.activehosted.com/f/1

As part of the malevolence-defeating paradigm, I have decided to focus on a multivariate approach by creating books on various topics connected to countering evil. I have made two mini-books focusing on leadership and mindset, designed to supplement and complement this book. To be a tyrant unto yourself, you need to be capable of leading yourself. Knowledge of leadership is thus vital. Please check out the Code of Champions and Master Virtue mini-books. I have given their links below.

https://www.amazon.com/CODE-CHAMPIONS-Greatest-Productivity-Performance-ebook/dp/B0B2RTVT8H

https://www.amazon.com/gp/product/B0B33J79Q1

If you have enjoyed this book, please consider leaving a 5-Star Review on Amazon. Reviews can help others find the book and more people will be able to benefit from this as you have. I would be extremely grateful for your honest feedback because it will help other folks to protect themselves from manipulation.

P.S:- Please feel free to talk to me at admin@www.phronesispublications.com or message me through the Facebook Group. I would love to hear from you!

Made in United States
Orlando, FL
15 September 2022